Albert Nelson Pate
(1934 – 2010)

You led the way by being my first example.
You encouraged my call into ministry from day one.
You challenged me to complete my final degree,
even when I didn't know if I could.
You always saw what was important.
Thanks, Dad!

(Philippians 3:13-14)

Table of Contents

Introduction

"S*tudents, what is the most important word in the English language?"* Dr. Oscar Thompson, my professor at Southwestern Seminary in Ft. Worth, Texas began his class on Vocational Evangelism the same way every morning. The first time he asked that question, I had no idea what the answer was. I thought of words like "love" or "grace," or even "faith." Fortunately, before any of us tried to respond in that very first class, he announced the answer. *"Relationships*...that's the most important word in the English language" he said.

As the semester passed, he continued to open class with the same question, and we learned to answer him in unison every morning. I guess that's called "good teaching" because the repetition burned that thought into my head. I never had another class with Dr. Thompson, but I never forgot about the most important word in the English language either!

Concentric Circles of Concern

Dr. Thompson died from cancer in 1980 after I graduated. His wife later compiled his class notes into a book, *Concentric Circles of Concern*, which explained Dr. Thompson's theory about evangelism flowing best along the lines of relationships. That is what he taught, what he believed, and what he practiced every day. In fact, he wrote, "When a society ceases to treasure relationships, it becomes decadent."[1] In the many years since I took his class, I have come to realize with a deep conviction how profoundly true all his teachings about relationships were and what significant application they have for the local church. No doubt, if a local church, or a Pastor, or a Deacon Body, or a Staff ever ceases to treasure relationships, decadence will set in. Spiritual life and congregational life will diminish, decay, dry up, and eventually die.

When one really stops to think about it, what word is more important in the English language than "relationships"? We can express and understand love, mercy, grace, (and all the other similar themes of Scripture) only in the context of relationships. Apart from the context of a real relationship, these powerful words are actually hollow and completely void of any meaning at all.

Evangelical Christians have forever stressed: "Salvation is a relationship" in contrast to merely a "religion." However, that's where we too often stop, leaving off Jesus' teaching about the second greatest commandment about our relationships *with others:* "You shall love your neighbor as yourself." (Matthew 22:39)

Dr. Thompson used a diagram he called "Concentric Circles of Concern" to illustrate his point about relationships and evangelism.[2] It was a set of concentric circles that represented the varying degrees of proximity a person shares with his/her family, friends, neighbors, co-workers, acquaintances and strangers. It's more likely that we will have opportunities to witness to those with whom we spend the most time relationally speaking (family, friends, etc.). In my ministry, I have used the idea of a target to capture the essence of what Dr. Thompson taught.

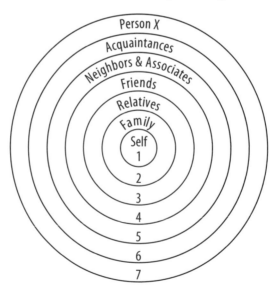

He encouraged us to pray for people in our "target" or concentric circles. First, he suggested we ask the Lord to show us any broken relationships that need mending. If He revealed a broken relationship, the prayer then became a request for the opportunity to reconcile.

The Problem with People

The problem is that people are not prone to want to deal with ruptured relationships. It's easier to think about Person X who needs to get right with Person Y. However, Dr. Thompson would insist that if we have ruptured relationships horizontally here on earth, we also have a ruptured relationship vertically with God in heaven.

I vividly remember a story he told about a student in his class named "Jim." One day when Dr. Thompson was teaching about the importance of reconciling with others, Jim blurted out, "Dr. Thompson, I have all kinds of problems with that." Dr. Thompson stopped his lecture and very gently asked Jim what was the matter. (Dr. Thompson was always very gracious with people who were angry, or who disagreed, or even those who argued.) Jim replied that he hadn't grown up in a Christian home and that his father had abandoned the family almost three decades prior. Jim said, "I am twenty-seven years old now, and I have never seen my father, and I don't want to see him."

Dr. Thompson responded, "Jim, I think you are in this class through divine providence. I think God is going to teach me something, you something, and this class something. Your father does not deserve forgiveness…but neither do you, and neither do I." He then shared a passage of Scripture on forgiveness (Matthew 6:14-15), which he proceeded to write on the blackboard. When he finished writing, there were actually tears in Jim's eyes as he softly asked, "But what should I do? I don't know where my father is. He may not even be alive."

Dr. Thompson wisely replied, "It doesn't matter. Take it to God, let Him tell you what to do, and leave it there. If God helps you find your father, you'll know what to do." He closed class that day with a specific prayer for Jim, and for all his students.

One day weeks later, Jim asked for the opportunity to share in class. Something had happened. Jim then related the story of how he had received two phone calls the same night. One was from his mom about an aunt who had died. Jim had always thought the aunt was his mother's sister because she had stayed close to the family after his father left. However, his mom explained that night that she was actually Jim's dad's sister. A little later, the second call came at Jim's house; it was his dad calling.

He asked for forgiveness and also told Jim that he had recently given his heart and life to Jesus Christ. He had heard that Jim was in seminary and asked if he could attend his graduation. Later that spring, Dr. Thompson and Jim's dad actually met.[3]

The truth from that experience illustrated what Dr. Thompson taught. If we are willing to reconcile our relationships, then the power of God will flow through our churches and result in miraculous answered prayer, dynamic spiritual growth in individuals, and in God-produced evangelism!

Despite Dr. Thompson's incredible influence on my life, I was a young man and I didn't think much about relationships or their importance. It took me years to realize just how significant Dr. Thompson's simple teaching was. First serving as a vocational evangelist and then later during my first pastorate, my focus was always on evangelism, discipleship, spiritual growth, God's will, the Word of God, morals, ethics, service, and truth. Emphasizing relationships just didn't fit into my pastoral agenda; nor did it fit into my program of preaching and teaching. Oh, how much I missed from the time I graduated from seminary in my twenties until the year I turned forty and faced a situation where I would find out just how important my seminary professor's lessons actually were.

CHAPTER 1

Crash Course in Relationships

In January of 1994, God challenged me to get out of my comfort zone. I had spent the previous ten years pastoring Northwood Baptist Church deep in the Piney Woods of Nacogdoches, Texas, with its tranquil setting among the forest and lakes. Home to Stephen F. Austin University (which had less than 10,000 students at the time), it was then also a small town of only 25,000. Imagine my surprise when God called me to pastor my second church, Northway Baptist in Angleton, Texas—a growing suburb of Houston, the fourth largest city in America.

The two churches shared a similar name, but that's where the similarities ended. They were as dramatically different as their locations. Instead of small town families, the membership at Angleton consisted of chemical plant engineers, workers, and leaders. We also had schoolteachers and other company employees, along with a few white-collar personnel. There was no strong college presence in the church like there had been at Northwood.

When I arrived at Angleton, I soon began to recognize a significant difference in my ministry time usage, too—especially in the area of pastoral counseling. In Nacogdoches, my focus was primarily on matters of discipleship, with some relationship issues occasionally mixed in. Now in the suburbs, I saw it was the reverse. I found myself at Northway spending the overwhelming majority of my counseling time (80-85%) working on relationships, those at home and those in the church. I had unknowingly signed up for a crash course in relationships!

Dynamics of Relationships

For the first time, I also began to consider how many vital lines of relationships there actually are in a church and how this profoundly affects a church's health and ministry. For example, there is the Pastor to People relationship, the Pastor to Staff relationship, the Staff to People relationship, and the Staff member to Staff member relationship. Things were changing all around me, and I began to wonder why. Several possibilities came to mind to account for the shift.

Society Is Always Changing

Society was rapidly changing in 1994, and that change was naturally being felt first in the larger population centers rather than in the rural settings like Nacogdoches. Mark Gerzon speaks about this trend in his book, *Leading Through Conflict*. He writes about the cultural changes invading our suburbs. "Walk down the street of an ordinary American town, such as Lincoln, Nebraska, and you will pass by Mohammed's Barber Shop, Jai'Jai's Hair Salon, and Pho's Vietnamese Café...This ordinary city, which both locals and outsiders often referred to as 'the middle of nowhere' is rapidly becoming 'the middle of *everywhere*.'" The author points out the importance of "leading across differences" in an age where dozens of cultures share the same city.[4] I could certainly attest to that, so I considered cultural changes as an explanation for the ministry shift I was experiencing.

No Two Churches Are Alike

The memberships of the two specific churches were radically different. In one, the college population demanded more discipleship-focused teaching. The students wanted to know what the Bible taught about God's will, the security of the believer, prayer, fasting, faith, temptation, witnessing, the purpose of the Church, and so much more. I was blessed to be involved in a ministry that helped students lay a biblical foundation for their beliefs to aid their future Christian living.

At Northway, discipleship was very important, too, but not on the scale of ministry in a "college town" local church. Maybe it was just the difference in the makeup of the two churches themselves that was creating this noticeable change in my ministry focus.

The Church Represents the World

The third possibility that came to me was that the Church as a whole in America in 1994 was beginning to reflect more of the "world." In other words, with the passing of time that occurred as my family moved from one church to the next, the problems that had once been considered more "outside" the Church had now moved "inside." Some would consider it an obvious compromise... the Church was becoming more "worldly," and the state of Christianity was in decline. That could be true.

Statistics presented during those days by leading researchers such as George Barna or Josh McDowell sure seemed to suggest that conclusion. We were often told that there existed only a "4% difference" between the moral behavior of those inside the Church and those outside.[5] The numbers were almost the same for the church member as the non-believer for divorce, frequency of pornography usage, fornication, adultery, and other moral value indicators. There was hardly any difference in the Church and the "world." Maybe that was the right explanation for what I was experiencing.

Deciding to Grow

Looking back, I believe that *all* of these were factors to a significant degree regarding the change in my ministry priorities. However, I also came to another and more important conclusion: It really didn't matter what was the cause! For the eternal sake of purposeful, God-Honoring, and relevant ministry as a Pastor, it was imperative that I grow, learn, and even change somewhat so that I could address the relational needs before me. I decided that the only way I would pass this crash course in relationships was to learn to confront biblically and to minister effectively in the church where I served and in the culture in which I lived. In the midst of navigating that challenge, I made a remarkable discovery about what God's Word says about relationships.

CHAPTER 2

A Surprising Discovery

Motivated by Dr. Thompson's admonition from years past, I began to dig into Scripture looking for relational truth. I couldn't help but be overwhelmed by the sheer volume of Scripture on this subject. There are literally tons of verses and passages in the Bible about relationships—in precept and principle—covering just about every kind of relationship imaginable! Work relationships, family relationships, government relationships, gender relationships and, most importantly to me as Pastor, church relationships—they are all mentioned in the Bible, and there's more besides. I guess I should not have been so surprised by this discovery since Christianity is first and foremost a "relationship," if it is anything at all. (See John 17:3, Matthew 22:36-38, Philippians 3:8.)

Second, I began to realize that the Bible presents healthy relationships as an indispensable key to healthy churches and powerful, effective ministry. This is not an optional, secondary suggestion. It is a priority, and it is mandatory. Likewise, being "relationship keepers" in the church is everyone's job—it is not just for the Pastor and Staff. I use that term to describe our role—making every effort to "keep the unity of the Spirit,"as the Bible says in Ephesians 4.

Let me illustrate what "Relationship Keeping" in a church looks like.

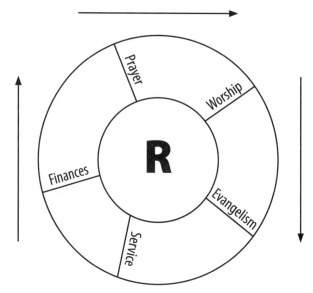

The hub in this illustration is central to the wheel. If it cracks or breaks, the whole wheel will collapse inwardly. The spokes are also important in supporting the wheel and enabling it to move forward (its intended purpose). The spokes must remain connected to the hub, in order to give the wheel full support.

Now, think of the wheel as representing a local church. The hub, which is so vital, represents Relationships in the Church. The spokes are the functions of a New Testament Church including prayer, worship, giving, evangelism, spiritual growth or Bible Study, and service.

I believe the Bible teaches that healthy relationships positively affect the functions of the Church. However, if the relationships aren't healthy, the functions won't be either. The "wheel" (Church) won't move forward or know real power. It could even collapse from within! John Maxwell summed it up with a single simple sentence: "We must get along to go along."[6]

A cursory look at just a few individual Bible verses will obviously support this important connection. Consider some of the key areas where the Bible connects the hub of Relationships with a particular function in the Church.

- **Worship...and Relationships** – Matthew 5:23-24
  "Therefore, if you are offering your gift at the altar *(in worship)* and then remember that your brother has something against you, leave your gift there in front of the altar. First go and be reconciled to your brother, and then come and offer your gift *(in an act of worship)*."
- **Prayer...and Relationships** – Psalm 66:18
  "If I had cherished sin *(in relationships)* in my heart, the Lord would not have listened *(to my prayer)*."
- **Evangelism...and Relationships** – John 17:20-21
  "My prayer is not for them alone. I pray also for those who will believe in me through their message, that all of them may be one *(unity in relationships)*, Father, just as you are in me and I in you. May they also be one in us so that the world may believe that you have sent me *(by this powerful unity in relationships)*." (See also John 13:35.)
- **Service...and Relationships** – 1 Corinthians 12:7, 12, 24-25
  "Now to each one the manifestation of the Spirit is given for the common good...*(service)* the body is a unit, though it is made up of many parts. God has combined the members of the body...so that there should be no division in the body *(relationships)*, but that its parts should have equal concern for each other."
- **Giving...and Relationships** – Acts 2:44-45
  "All the believers were together *(physically)* and had everything in common *(possessions/relationships)*. Selling their possessions and goods, they gave to anyone as he had need." *(a new relationship to people and possessions)*.
- **Spiritual Growth...and Relationships** – Acts 2:42
  "They were continually devoting themselves to the apostles' teaching and to fellowship..."

Christian Leaders Speak

Clearly, the Bible has a lot to teach us in the context of our relationships with others. However, I'm not the first or only one to make this discovery. Many well-known and well-respected Christian leaders have spoken about the importance of healthy relationships in the Church and the powerful connection between them and the carrying out of basic church functions and ministries.

RELATIONSHIP KEEPERS

CHAPTER 3

Leaders Speak

A
t Saddleback Church in California, the mission statement is: "A Great Commitment to the Great Commission and the Great Commandment will grow a Great Church!" Part of that "Great Commandment" is to love others. That represents a commitment to healthy relationships, and it is a guiding principle for the ministries and functions of that great church led by Pastor Rick Warren.

Warren goes even further by implying that authentic discipleship and spiritual growth can *only* take place in the context of healthy relationships. He notes that too much Christian teaching is self-centered, without reference to our relationships with others. He writes, *"Christians need relationships to grow... The quality of your relationship to Christ can be seen in the quality of your relationship to other believers."*[7]

In my study, I began to see that Warren and other Christian leaders often tied together the church function of evangelism (among unbelievers) with healthy church relationships (among believers). For example, many Christians can't relate to unbelievers for the purpose of evangelism because they never learned how to relate in a healthy way to Christians first!

My response to that is simply, "Amen and Amen!" Most of us hear bits and pieces of what Scripture teaches about relationships; entire messages regarding relationships are rarely developed with the exception of popular passages like 1 Corinthians 13 on love or Ephesians 5-6 on the family. We have also heard *some* teaching on important attitudes we should have in our relationships, including things like humility, acceptance, forgiveness, love, or deference, but seldom have we been taught healthy relationship principles or the connection between healthy relationships and effectiveness in the basic functions of a church. That may be why the priority on building and maintaining healthy relationships in the local church has been absent. In contrast, Chip Ingram, CEO of Walk Thru the Bible Ministries, goes so far as to say that relationships are actually God-ordained as the primary way we learn.[8]

Service

Likewise, our spiritual gifts for service are not for ourselves but for the benefit and edification of others in the Body of Christ. That can only occur through the medium of congregational relationships, whether that takes place in one-on-one settings, in small groups, or in a corporate gathering. Dr. Jack MacGorman in his book, *The Gifts of the Spirit*, draws a similar conclusion in his exposition of 1 Corinthians 12-14. He writes, "The gifts of the Holy Spirit are bestowed upon each individual for the benefit of the entire congregation. They are not adornment for our private benefit, but rather anointment for our joint service. Though the bestowal is individual, the benefit is congregational."[9]

Later in the same book, MacGorman emphasizes how healthy relationships result in effective service through the use of spiritual gifts. He proposes that the Early Church as a whole made strides whenever believers ignored economic, social and ethnic distinctions that kept people apart and instead chose to override them with Christian unity. However, he points out that the specific congregation in Corinth struggled with relational unity, and their ability to do ministry suffered as a result. He writes, "Disparities as race, gender, vocation, politics, economics and age could all make it difficult to establish and maintain true community in our troubled world. Yet, in Christ, these diversities lose their power to divide…In Corinth, however, this was hardly so. In the constant rivalry and contention that existed, church solidarity *(relationships)* was violated, and the capacity to function *(in service)* as the Body of Christ was threatened."[10]

Relational Discipleship

Jim Putman is the Senior Pastor of Real Life Ministries Church in Post Falls, Idaho. Jim is a former All-American Collegiate wrestler, and he has written two books including *Church is a Team Sport*. Post Falls is almost in the middle of nowhere with a population of approximately 10,000 people (although there are over 100,000 people within a 25-mile radius). RLM began in the summer of 1998 with only four families. It then grew to 50 people in a little over two months and held its first official service in October of 1998 with 142 people present. Within three years, God grew this church from four families to 2,300 people! Today, RLM is one of the fastest growing churches in America, averaging over 8,000 in weekly attendance and 600-plus weekly small groups.

What is the foundation to a successful church like Real Life Ministries? In a word, it is *relationships*. In the foreword to Jim's first book, Avery Willis attributes small groups to RLM's success. He writes, "[RLM leaders] believe that you can't make disciples in a vacuum such as a class where you just pass on information… In every large worship service, the leaders emphasize that people must get connected to a small group in order to grow."[11] Putman adds an emphasis on "shepherding" the people. If a church member was missing, they called to follow up. When someone was sick, they prayed and helped where they could. Putman writes, "We believed in *relational* discipleship. When someone came to the Lord, they needed someone to walk with them; they needed to be taught."[12]

Putman tells of a crossroads the church faced when the numbers were growing, and the Pastors were struggling to keep up the pace. Jim writes, "Success was killing us. But we knew in our hearts this wasn't success. We were on our way to losing. We were becoming a show."[13]

The turning point came when the leadership team decided not to be like other big churches. They presented a different plan to their congregation for their future. The plan was to deemphasize "the show" and focus on shepherding, discipleship, and *relationships*. The people attending RLM were encouraged to become ministers, not merely spectators.

This change of direction was a result of Putman searching his own heart and life as the Senior Pastor. When the problem first arose, he did what any young Pastor in a fast-growing church would do. He began visiting other similar churches to talk with their Pastors to learn what to do next.

He describes having lengthy conversations with some of the Pastors but feeling more confused afterward. After talking with them, Putman decided his view of success was entirely different from theirs. While some of the Pastors of larger churches pointed to "numbers and formulas and buildings and radio programs" as a means of success, Putman felt that something was missing. "I didn't hear about *relationships*," he writes. " I heard a lot about the show on the weekends, how to use video projectors, or how to tweak the worship service to really draw a crowd. The buildings I visited were probably full on the weekend, but they were like cemeteries during the week. As I walked away from those many meetings, I once again believed that the team was losing in most places. Even in many churches that appeared to be winning, we were getting drilled."[14] In the end, Putman decided that God is calling people into a sincere and real relationship with Him—and with others as well.

I know what Pastor Putman is talking about, and as a Christian leader you probably do, too. Without a focus on real life and relationships, not much gets done for the Kingdom—no matter how successful we appear on the outside. We can have well-attended churches that have perfected the methods to draw a crowd. There are plenty of seminars to choose from on how to tweak your worship services to increase your attendance. However, I believe it's time for the Church to uphold a new model for success and listen to another message—one that focuses on relationships. Much of what we know about the practical application of relationship principles comes from an unlikely source: the business world. What can the Church learn from it? You might be surprised.

CHAPTER 4

The Church Needs to Listen

In the business world, healthy relationships between companies and customers, executives and employees, have long been touted as a priority. If a leader (or a business for that matter) wanted to be successful, almost every business book included a focus on the centrality of relationships.

A New Model

In the modern business world, a new prototype for the world-class leader has emerged, one who is seen as the symbol of the kind of leadership that our world needs most today. It's the mediator. The mediator is that person who sees conflict as an unavoidable reality and a natural expression of our changing world today. To the mediator, conflict in relationships cannot be ignored, denied, or avoided. The mediator/leader views our world as one of inevitable division and difference. Our world is "coming together" through advances in technology and travel like never before and our values and cultures are colliding. The mediator even considers conflict as an essential test of leadership today, an "opportunity" for learning that can lead to positive transformation in our relationships, enterprises, and institutions. To the mediator, it's not so much a matter of trying to understand or prevent the causes of conflict and division. What's important is handling the conflict for the sake of greater growth and the benefit of all involved. To that end, the new business world literature insists that world-class business leaders must develop the skills for turning differences into opportunities—or they simply won't succeed.

Nelson Mandela is one of the most admired leaders in our world today. He represents this mediator style of leadership on a worldwide scale. Mandela spent a quarter century behind bars as a victim of apartheid in South Africa. He writes in his autobiography, *Long Walk to Freedom*, of wanting freedom only for himself at first, but then his desire to be free progressed to include everyone who "looked like I did." Finally, he wanted freedom for everyone regardless of race, tribe, or stature. He wrote: "My hunger for the freedom of my *own* people became a hunger for the freedom of all people. I knew as well as I knew anything that the oppressor must be liberated, just as surely as the oppressed. A man who takes away (another) man's freedom is a prisoner of hatred, and is locked behind the bars of his prejudice…both are robbed of their humanity. When I walked out of prison, that was my mission: to liberate the oppressed and the oppressor both."[15] Mandela became a "cross-boundary" leader, a man who was not stopped by differences or obstacles in relationships but learned how to effectively lead across these!

Scan a list of successful businesses today, and the value statements of these companies will all reflect a clear commitment to healthy relationships. For example, one secular corporation lists three values:

1. **Respect for People**
2. **Responsibility for Actions and Results**
3. **Relationships with Each Other**: Our success is built on quality relationships. We communicate openly and truthfully in a timely manner.

   We encourage constructive feedback. We are committed to each other and have fun together. We are helpful and compassionate. We treat others the way we want to be treated.[16]

These three commitments sound like great values for any and every church, don't they? Indeed, they sound almost "biblical." I believe God would very much approve of their formula for "success," especially that third value. To God, success is measured in terms of a healthy relationship with Him and healthy relationships with His people. (See John 17:3, Philippians 3:1-10, and 1 John 4:7-11.) A case in point is Acts 2 where we learn how the Early Church members treated each other.

"Those who accepted his message...were added to their number that day...they devoted themselves...to the fellowship...all the believers were together...they gave to anyone who had need...every day they continued to meet together...they ate together with glad and sincere hearts... enjoying the favor of all the people..." (vs. 41-47)

I like how another highly successful company, the R. W. Beckett Corporation, listed six guiding principles for its employees. Larry Julian included these in his book, *God Is MY CEO*, as examples of corporate leadership. The six principles include: Focus, People, Conduct, Work Environment, Stewardship, and Citizenship. "We build and maintain solid relationships of respect among ourselves, our customers, and our suppliers, encouraging the growth and well-being of each employee."[17]

This particular company strongly encourages family relationships with its employees and has gone so far as to back up their beliefs with actual policies that are relationship-driven. For example, a percentage of paid maternity leave is provided for up to 26 weeks. This company also provides a $1,000 adoption benefit. In addition, they host open houses and company visits for all, and family members and relatives are favorably considered for employment with the company.

Ken Blanchard, considered one of the forefront leadership consultants worldwide for the past 30-plus years, has similar guiding principles for his company. He is the author of numerous books including his phenomenal bestseller, *The One Minute Manager,* which sold over 13 million copies. Blanchard's impact has been extraordinary on the national and international level. Today, he is the Chief Spiritual Officer of the Ken Blanchard Companies, a training and consulting firm. Blanchard lists four operating values for his companies:
1. **Ethical** – Doing the right thing.
2. **Relationships** – Developing mutual trust and respect.
3. **Success** – Operating a profitable and well-run organization.
4. **Learning** – Always growing, inquiring, and developing.

He clearly states, "We won't do anything to improve the profitability of the company that is unethical, *or that doesn't honor the relationships* we have with our customers, our people, our suppliers, and our community...Your treatment of people is leadership in action. Great leaders value both results and *relationships*. Both are critical for long term survival and success.[18]

Why?

Why has the Church (especially in America) not understood and learned these principles long ago? Maybe we did hold to it once, but in the midst of progress, growth, advancement, industrialization, and technological explosion, the emphasis on relationships seems to have changed or been lost altogether. The Church began to lose its way when it started reflecting the often impersonal Western society and culture in which we live. We began experiencing consequences such as individual loneliness, isolation, separation, results-orientation, institutionalism, loss of identity, and a factory or corporation mindset.

Leaders in the Church have known about the importance of relationships, and yet there is a disconnect when that priority has not really been addressed in our training. However, relationships in the local church are not secondary; they are a priority. I consider select leaders such as the Pastor, Staff, and Deacons/Elders as the "Relationship Gatekeepers" in their local church Body. They are to model good relationships by example and exhortation.

A New Job Description

Church Leaders sometimes tend to think of their core responsibilities as limited to management, decision-making, finances and funding, personnel, programming, education, maintenance, and long-range planning. Sure, there are also added spiritual priorities of prayer, evangelism, missions, bereavement, pastoral care, and stewardship.

But what about building and maintaining healthy *relationships?* The Church is not made of brick and mortar; the Church is not organizations and meetings. The Church is people, and the most crucial issue of the Church is, therefore, relationships. Do you see yourself as the catalyst, equipper and protector of healthy relationships in your Church Family? Are you the Gatekeeper? Is that part of your "charge," too? If that is your desire, let's spend some time understanding what this new job description looks like and how it functions.

The Bible presents some clear relational instructions, in principle and precept, that can radically increase the effectiveness of any leader or church. There are probably many others, but I want to present four of the most simple and direct guidelines for shepherding relationships below:

1. We must learn to **appeal** to one another, not **attack** one another, when there is difference, disagreement, offense, or division.
2. We must learn **to** communicate and **how** to communicate.
3. We must **learn** and **live** true loyalty in the Body of Christ.
4. We must **care** enough to **confront** sin or error, in belief or behavior in the family of faith.

My experience as a church Pastor for 23 years helped me to assimilate these time-tested principles from the Bible. The next few chapters will unpack each Guideline and show you how to incorporate these truths into your own leadership situation so you can be more effective.

CHAPTER 5

Guideline One: Appeal, Not Attack

We must learn to **appeal** to one another, not **attack** one another, when there is difference, disagreement, offense, or division.

Focal Passage:

"And the *servant* of the Lord must not *strive*, but be *gentle* with all men, *apt to teach, patient*, in *meekness instructing* those that oppose him, if God will perhaps give them repentance to the acknowledging of the truth, and that they may *recover* themselves out of the snare of the devil, who are taken captive by him at his will (to do his will)." 2 Timothy 2:24-26 KJV (emphasis added)

L et's begin by looking at the key words and concepts in this focal passage from 2 Timothy that show how leaders are to treat those under their care. Some simple definitions might help:

1. "Servant": Anyone who knows Christ, the people in the pew, in the pulpit, and on the platform. The word is *doulos* or "slave," a person under the command of his master with no will or rights of his own. We all have a responsibility in relationships.
2. "Strive": The word means to quarrel, argue, or fight. The Amplified translation uses the word "contending." The reason for some of the problems in relationships is the tendency to defend our pride, position, or power. We compete and attack.

3. "Gentle": The word is best translated "kind to all."
4. "Apt to Teach": An able teacher, one who is skilled, ready.
5. "Patient": The NIV reads, "not resentful." But the NASV translation reads, "patient when wronged." The idea of this word is actually being ready and willing to bear poor treatment *without* getting resentful. I can't help but think of the movie character, Forest Gump, who won so many people over with his innocence, simplicity, and willingness to endure wrong and not retaliate in word or deed. This was especially true between Gump and his army lieutenant whose life he saved and who later became his business partner and best man. The lieutenant treated Gump harshly throughout the movie, but Gump remained understanding and supportive without a hint of resentment, and they became best friends.
6. "Meekness": Self under control. The expression of gentleness and courtesy.
7. "Oppose": Think of "opposition" or an opponent.
8. "Recover": "Escape" is the word used by the NIV and NASV translations. The word actually describes a man coming out of a drunken stupor. Satan makes people drunk with his lies, and the servant's task is to sober them up and rescue them (false teachers and false doctrine). [19]

In this passage, the Apostle Paul is speaking about believers and Christian leaders who are in a position of teaching others. However, they are teaching false information and false doctrine. The people being taught may have been those inside the Church, or outside. Regardless, these teachers are displaying an obvious opposition to the truth. Paul gives direction on the proper response of God's servant to the opponent and the opposition.

The specific cause for conflict in this passage is doctrinal truth. However, it could just as easily be a difference of ideas, preferences, or personal opinions and feelings. Whatever the conflict in the Church is, the *approach* to the problem needs to be the same. Notice *the strong, positive relational approach* indicated by the words "gentle or kind," "patient or forbearing," "meekness or courtesy," and "instructing or gentle correcting." These speak of an honest, earnest **appeal** for resolution to the problem.

In contrast, Paul says God's servants are not to "strive" in their efforts to resolve this conflict. The word "strive" as it is used here is the word of **attack**. It carries the idea of contending, opposing, arguing, fighting, or quarreling. Picture two sides of a debate or a fight. There is a winner and a loser. The goal of each "opponent" in the debate is victory, mastery, domination, or control over the other. There is no thought of reconciliation or the "recovery" of the relationship. The relationship is not even important for consideration. In a debate, what is important is the subject of disagreement, not the two people in the disagreement or their relationship to each other. Regarding debates and disagreements, Dr. Warren Wiersbe comments to the contrary: "A servant's purpose is not to win arguments, but to win souls."[20]

Appeal vs. Attack

Let's look more closely at some of the contrasts I would like to suggest that exist between an Appeal and an Attack.

> **Appeal** – A person speaks truth to another but with respect and regard for the other person. The words are directed toward *performance* (action or choices) or beliefs.

> **Attack** – A person speaks truth to another, but with disrespect and disregard for the person. The words are directed toward a *person* and his/her worth, identity, or character.

- In an **attack**, truth is a *weapon*. In an **appeal**, truth is a <u>tool</u>. *Ask yourself:*
  - Do I tear down or build up?
  - Do I seek to defeat and destroy, or develop?
  - Do I aim to help or hurt?

  Some weapons can be tools, and most tools can be weapons. Truth needs to be used as both an offensive *weapon* against Satan, and a helpful *tool* in people's lives!

- In an **attack**, I become the Judge. In an **appeal**, *God* alone is the Judge. *One who judges:*
  - …condemns without seeking to help or resolve.
  - …forms opinions and conclusions on first impressions or hearsay.
  - …is eager to tell others about a person's failures.

- ...focuses upon motives rather than action (the "why" more than the "what") thus attacking someone's character.

- In an **attack**, I assume I know all the *facts*. In an **appeal**, I assume I don't know all the facts and must learn what actually happened.
  Ask yourself:
  - Have I checked the accuracy of all facts and factors?
  - Is my "evidence" out of context?

- In an **attack**, *points* are more important. In an **appeal**, *people* are more important. You may win an argument and lose a relationship or more! Winning an argument is not worth it if you negatively affect your church health, future opportunities, and general progress. Instead of *competing* with others, seek to *complete* others. Following Christ's example, we see that the goal is not to *surpass* all others whatever the cost, but to *serve* all others whatever the cost.

I like what Dr. Duane Litfin notes on this text in 2 Timothy regarding the inevitable consequences of false teaching and also the proper relationship response in a church. He writes, "False teaching will always be divisive, but the Lord's servant should not be a fighter, but a promoter of unity. The goal is always remedial, not punitive, when dealing with brothers. The purpose must always be to edify Christ's body, not tear it down. When a brother falls into false teaching, he must be treated with gentleness and Christian love. False teaching and all its negative consequences in the church are always the handiwork of Satan, but God in His grace often salvages the situation through the *Christ-like ministry* of His servants." [21]

Points of Application from 2 Timothy 2

What Contributes to an Attack
The servant of the Lord knows there will be conflicts in relationships (v.25).

1. Human Nature
Unfortunately, it's not a case of "if" but "when" there will be opposition in the Church. According to this passage, it seems to be accepted and assumed that it will happen. How do we know that? For several reasons, but certainly because common sense tell us that "people will be people." Remember, the middle letter of the word "sin" is "I." Selfishness, selfness, and the problem of pride are present in all people and will surely cause disagreement, opposition, conflict, and broken relationships. Offenses are just as inevitable as is sin. (Matthew 18:7) A prayer every believer needs to constantly pray is John 3:30: "**I** must decrease, but **He** must increase."

2. Immaturity
There is also the contributing factor of differing maturity levels within the Body of Christ. In a family, those levels of maturity contribute to fights, misunderstandings, impatience, disharmony, and even retribution. Likewise, the Church is not fully mature. As growing children, we share different perspectives, so conflicts will arise.

Still, Paul's admonition in 1 Thessalonians 5:13-24 applies:

"…Live in **peace** with each other. We urge you, brethren, admonish the **unruly**, encourage the **fainthearted**, help the **weak**, be **patient** with everyone (in the Family). See that no one repays **another** with evil for evil, but always seek after that which is **good** for one **another** and for all people. Rejoice always; Pray without ceasing; In everything give thanks, for this is God's will for you in Christ Jesus. Do not quench the Spirit; do not despise prophetic utterances. But examine everything carefully; hold fast to that which is good; abstain from every form of evil. Now may the God of **peace** Himself sanctify you entirely; may your spirit and soul and body be preserved complete, without blame at the coming of our Lord Jesus Christ. Faithful is He who calls you, and He will also bring it to pass." NASV

Taken alone, these are great individual exhortations to believers for all times. However, notice how much the passage reads like a final checklist of instructions that a parent would give to his/her children before leaving on a night out. Knowing the children's maturity levels are not the same, a wise parent leaves a warning because conflict is likely going to happen.

3. Spiritual Diversity
Conflicts are also to be expected if for no other reason than because of our spiritual *diversity*. In passages like Ephesians 4, Romans 12, and 1 Corinthians 12, we are told of an intentional *spiritual* diversity that God Himself created in the giving of spiritual gifts! In other words, on top of a diversity of race, background, nationality, skill, gender, and personality that already exists, God throws into the Body of Christ another level of differences for us to experience and manage. God loves diversity, and the lesson for us is to love it, too. We must learn to be complemented by it and value it, not react to it or try to conform and change it.

A lot of people like to criticize and dismiss the Church because of the disagreement, discord, and disharmony that sometimes exists. (As if the Church should be perfect and free from any relationship conflicts.) Some feel that the presence of something "negative" is a justifiable excuse to reject the Church, its message, and its Redeemer. Truly, that is quite the "excuse" and nothing more. God's Word never teaches or promises perfect unity and peace in the local church this side of eternity. A church is a *family*, and even very *healthy* families are "relationship challenged" periodically. A family *grows* through these challenging times, if handled properly.

God is not looking for a *perfect* church or a church at *perfect peace*. He is looking for believers who are forever committed to one another and mature enough to follow His ways for building and living *healthy* relationships, not the world's ways, or man's ways. God will make His ways known. (Psalm 103:7) The true challenge for any local church is not to remove all sources of conflict and relationship disharmony but to resolve these correctly and biblically when such occur. That is maturity, love, and Christianity in action!

Fight for People, Not Against Them

The servant of the Lord is fighting for people, not against *people...especially those in the family of faith. (v.26)*

Notice the phrase Paul uses to describe the purpose of dealing with conflict: "...that they may recover" from a snare of the devil. People who have been ensnared, trapped, or taken captive by deceit or error are *not* the enemy; Satan is the enemy. Satan is at work in the deception of an individual and the division in a relationship. The right perspective for the servant of the Lord is operating a "recovery mission."

Imagine a young married couple having problems in their relationship. Let's say they approach their respective parents for help. Wise parents don't take sides unless there has been abuse or infidelity. Instead, they take the "side" of the marriage itself. It's not "his" side or "her" side but "<u>their</u>" side that matters most. Wise parents come alongside the young couple and help them work together for the same goal: saving their marriage!

In like manner, the Christian leader sees his/her role as not working against the opposing people but working in their behalf *against* Satan. This is the Heavenly Father's "vantage" point, and it is the right one. If repentance results and recovery occurs, then reconciliation in a relationship will result, too. It's time to think "Family" and think of each other in terms of "us," not "them," when it comes to addressing conflict in our churches. The right perspective leads to the right actions, words, purposes, emotions, and approach. How do you see the people in your church?

Gain Control of the Situation

The servant of the Lord gains control instead of losing control.

The control needed is not of others, but of oneself. Notice the words again in the first two verses of the focal passage: gentle, apt to teach, and patient. Think especially of the word "meekness." This word refers to strength under control. It is a picture of a person who is able to yield personal rights, pride, and position. It's not a natural character trait, or learned etiquette. It is a fruit of the Spirit in a godly believer's life.

Control is very important in relational healing and re-building. Without it, we go against others with our emotions. With control, we gravitate toward them instead. In other words, a person can attack another with their emotions, as well as their words.

In doing so, a person can lose a relationship, an opportunity for growth, a personal testimony of God's healing power, and so much more. If people are out of control when they approach others regarding a problem, they are very likely to turn what was initially a proverbial molehill into a mountain between them.

Communicate Well
The servant of the Lord realizes that proper communication is a key to healthy relationships. (v.25) Notice v.25 says "instructing." That means providing guidance or leadership to another. It is not the idea of lecturing.

Make Recovery Your Goal
The servant of the Lord's goal for broken relationships is recovery and reconciliation. (vs.25-26)
There can be no reconciliation in some relationships without repentance and recovery of the truth. Of first importance is a person's relationship with God. Without repentance and recovery of the truth, reconciliation to God is impossible. The relationship with God is first and foremost in importance to the servant of the Lord. The byproduct is restored relationships with people.

The goal in relationships is not pride, position, and power. It is not about personal satisfaction gained at another's expense or gaining strokes for a poor self-esteem. In 2 Timothy 2, the servant of the Lord may have been hurt, even deeply, but he/she is not hurting back. The goal in relationships is to make everyone a winner instead of one person a winner, and one person a loser. When there is a winner and a loser in relationships both people actually lose to a degree. There are ways to create the opportunity for all to win, although it may not be easy. Even then, the outcome is not guaranteed by any means, but at least the bridge has been built and people in opposition to each other have a choice to cross over it.

Teach, Don't Triumph
The servant of the Lord's focus in relationships is to teach and train people, not triumph over them.
Although this is the last in my list, it is actually the first priority. When there are relationship conflicts, it's time to listen for God, think/meditate on Scripture, ask and search for His wisdom

(Proverbs 2, James 1:5), pray, and then allow God's Spirit to reveal the next step. There is no manual to guide us through every individual situation. However, for the one who will hear His voice and obey, there is a way to treasure relationships through an **appeal** method and not trash them through **attacks**!

Understanding Communication Is Key

Howard Raiffa once wrote, "In most conflicts, the main part of the problem...consists in getting people to talk and to listen to one another."[22]

In the next chapter, we'll learn how you can guide the communication process in the midst of a conflict so that both parties reach resolution. People need to commit themselves to talk and listen when conflict or problems in relationships arise. They also need to know how to communicate correctly, or the problems can get worse.

Talking Points

Guideline #1: We must learn how to appeal to people, not attack people.

1. In an attack, truth is a weapon. In an appeal, truth is a tool.
   Ask:
   - Do I tear down or build up? Do I seek to defeat, destroy, or develop?
2. In an attack, I become the Judge. In an appeal, God alone is the Judge.
   Ask:
   - Do I condemn without seeking to help or resolve? Do I form opinions on first impressions or hearsay? Am I eager to tell others about a person's failure?
3. In an attack, I assume I know all the facts. In an appeal, I assume I don't.
   Ask:
   - Have you checked the accuracy of all facts and factors? Is "evidence" out of context?
4. In an attack, points are more important. In an appeal, people are more important.
   Ask:
   - Is it more important to me to win an argument, or keep a relationship? Do I complete others instead of competing against them?

The Servant of the Lord in Relationships:

1. The Servant of the Lord knows there will be conflicts in relationships. Why is this a reality?
2. The Servant of the Lord realizes he/she is fighting for people, not against people. In what ways can you fight for people in your congregation?
3. The Servant of the Lord gains control instead of losing control. How difficult is it for you to hold your temper?
4. The Servant of the Lord realizes that proper communication is a key to healthy relationships. Why is that true?
5. The Servant of the Lord's goal for broken relationships is recovery and reconciliation. What is your experience with recovery and reconciliation?

CHAPTER 6

Guideline Two: Communication

We must learn *to* communicate and *how* to communicate.

Focal Passages:

"Speaking the truth in love…" Ephesians 4:15

"Brothers, if someone is caught in a sin (fault, KJV), you who are spiritual should restore him gently (meekness, KJV). But watch yourself, or you may also be tempted." Galatians 6:1 (parentheses added)

"If your brother sins against you, go and show (by words) him his fault, just between the two of you. If he listens to you, you have won your brother over. But if he will not listen, take one or two others along…" Matthew 18:15-16 (parentheses added)

Healthy relationships are *born, built,* and *blessed* through healthy communication. However, don't confuse talking only, or talking more, with "communication." Talking is not necessarily communication. Neither is debating. One person may not talk as much as another person does. The Bible actually cautions us to "be swift to hear, and slow to speak." (James 1:19) It also says, "In the multitude of words, there lacketh not sin, and he that refraineth his lips is wise." (Proverbs 10:19 KJV)

As a Pastor, Evangelist, and Director of Missions, I have

often joked that I "make my living with my mouth." For that reason it is good to pray daily, "Set a watch, O Lord, before my mouth. Keep the door of my lips." (Psalm 141:3 KJV) "Let the words of my mouth and the meditation of my heart be acceptable in Thy sight, O Lord, my strength and my Redeemer." (Psalm 19:14 KJV)

Healthy Communication

My wife and her stepmother have the "gift of gab," so to speak. My father-in-law used to look at me with a wink and a smile whenever they got together and say, "Neither one of them is listening to the other. One is just re-loading while the other one is firing."

Alan Kobane said, "If we want to change the world, we have to change ourselves—including how we talk and listen.[23] The elements of healthy communication include key words like listening, talking, hearing, feeling, respect, and practicing sensitivity. We need to listen carefully and patiently to hear what is said and what is meant. We must demonstrate respect for another person's opinion and perspective and show sensitivity and feeling for the other person's emotions. When it is our turn to talk, it helps to take an appropriate tone, watch the length of our turn talking, and choose the right setting for the conversation to take place.

We often think of leaders as being eloquent speakers—but listening is actually the greater skill. Mark Gerzon describes world class "mediator leaders," such as Nelson Mandela, as having a "deep commitment to first hearing what others have to say. While they may be powerful speakers, what makes them so effective is not their tongues but their ears."[24]

Dr. Chip Ingram wrote a book entitled, *Good to Great in God's Eyes*. In that book, Ingram mentions a lesson he learned about what makes a great marriage. He writes, "I learned one thing from [another author's book] that transformed my marriage: talking is not communicating. Communication is the meeting of meanings."[25] He is referring to feelings, thoughts, ideas, and desires that are beneath the words we actually speak.

Dr. John Maxwell gives some great listening helps in his book, *Developing the Leader Within You*.[26] He even has a quiz to test yourself to see if you are a good listener. He asks things like: Do you interrupt others? Do you get agitated when you disagree with someone? How easily can you tune out distractions? Being a good listener is hard work!

To help you evaluate your listening skills, let a close friend or family member evaluate you and give you feedback. Ask how well you handle distractions…are you able to stay focused? Inquire about how well you seem to control your emotions in the midst of tense conversations.

Problems in Communication
Paul Tillich once wrote, "The first duty of love is to listen."[27] There seems to be two primary problems when it comes to healthy communication in a church.
- Some know *how* to communicate, but they hesitate!
- Some don't hesitate, but they don't know *how* to communicate!

In one of our focal passages, Ephesians 4:15, we learn what it means to "speak the truth in love." Let's unpack that phrase from the Bible word by word.

Key Word #1 – Speak
There is a time to speak and a need for us to speak. What can and will often hurt relationships is people who *won't* speak, who *choose* not to speak, who *refuse* to speak or who are too *busy* to speak.

The old proverbial saying, "Silence is golden" is well known. However, is that actually true? The answer is both "true" and "false."

- **It's True** – When you've talked yourself to death or been talked to death all day.
- **It's True** – When you've been in a noisy environment all day.
- **It's True** – When saying things you can't take back.
- **It's True** – When talking too much would convince others you are not the brightest light bulb in the building. Proverbs 17:28 says, "Even a fool is thought wise if he keeps silent, and discerning if he holds his tongue."

BUT

Silence is not golden when you are:
- Trying to build healthy relationships.
- Restoring a brother from failure/sin/fault.
- Reconciling an offense.

People are sometimes guilty of actually "using" silence in a non-biblical, disobedient manner. We all know silence is valuable and can be very healthy for individuals and relationships, but what can be used for good is too often used for bad in many areas of life. For example, Scripture clearly states that retribution or revenge toward an offender when one is hurt is the sole responsibility of the Lord. (Romans 12:17-21) It is not an individual believer's right to give the "silent treatment" to punish someone else. At times people use silence as a technique to get even or get back at someone who has hurt them. Their thought process is something like, "I am mad at you. You hurt me. I don't like you. You offended me. So, I won't talk to you. That's how I will treat you...and that's how I will get even." Not speaking to another person becomes a control technique or even a "weapon" of retribution and revenge.

Being silent (not speaking) is good when the time of quiet is used for prayer, reflection, study, or self-control. It is wrong, however, when it is used to hurt, embarrass, or punish another. There are several additional reasons why people refuse to speak to one another:

- Emotional Hurt. This is very understandable. People need time and silence to heal. The danger is keeping the pain within for too long, resulting in bitterness and unresolved anger.
- Avoidance. This is the fear of conflict and confrontation.
- Pride. This is essentially telling the other person, "You speak first...then maybe I will."

I once asked a couple who divorced after 30 years of marriage what happened. The simple and oft-heard reply was, "No communication." There are two wonderful examples in Scripture of someone communicating their way through a problem with successful results.

God's Example – Read Hebrews 1:1-2; Romans 5:8
The Bible says in Romans 5:8 that God demonstrated (and still demonstrates) His love for us in that even while we were sinners, Jesus died for us. In other words, even when we mistreated, hurt, and offended Him, He still showed love toward us by His *actions* (sending Jesus).

If you add the thought of Hebrews 1:1-2 to this truth, there is another layer of application for this lesson. The passage in Hebrews says God spoke to people throughout history in many ways, and He continues to speak to people until this day. Even though He has been wounded by humanity's unbelief, rebellion, and rejection, He never stopped talking to us.

God could have given us the silent treatment. He could have refused to speak, but instead He demonstrated His love for us by *speaking* to us through His Son, the One known as the very "Word" of God. People may give people the "silent" treatment, but thank God He didn't and never will!

Nehemiah's Example – Read Nehemiah 5:6-13 KJV
In this story from the Bible, the people under Nehemiah's responsibility and leadership were not treating each other right. They had a major relationship problem that hindered the work they were doing in the Lord's name (rebuilding the wall of Jerusalem). Nehemiah became very angry and withdrew to "consult with himself." He then took several important steps in communication:

- He *spoke* to the people directly involved. Note: There are only two reasons to speak to others outside a situation. To do otherwise is to gossip, judge, or slander.
  1. **To Gain Insight** – Focus on the process (not the person) to learn the best approach and any additional facts which will help in restoration.
  2. **To Get Involvement** – to request the assistance of others to help, not hurt, in the actual approach.
- He spoke to the responsible parties only after he took time to *process*. (Gained control of himself)
- He spoke the *truth in love.*

As a result of these steps, the response to what he said was ideal. The people *repented* of their selfishness, they made *restitution*, and they *restored* healthy relationships in the congregation. The final affirmation of the people in verse 13 when the conflict was resolved was a unified and hearty "Amen!"

Key Word #2 – Truth
Here is where we fail many times. First, we need to realize there are at least two kinds of truth. There is the truth people speak regarding

the *facts*, and the truth they speak regarding their *feelings*.

- **Facts** – objective, clear, observable evidence
- **Feelings** – subjective responses, reactions, and perspective

Examples of Facts-Truth: "This was what happened..."

"This is what I saw/heard..."

"This is what I said/did..."

Examples of Feelings-Truth: "This is what I felt…"

"This is how that made me feel..."

"This is what I perceived…"

    Both of these types of truth operate legitimately in our relationships. Someone may be speaking one or the other or both in one conversation. It helps to clarify, identify and understand where a person is coming from—facts, feelings or both.

    It's important in resolving conflicts to speak the truth and make clear what kind of truth we are speaking. How someone "feels" may be genuine, but it may not be based on accurate or complete information. Henry W. Longfellow once said, "If we could read the secret history of others, we should find in each man's life sorrow and suffering enough to disarm us of all hostility."[28] Someone's *feelings* toward another or about a situation may be true, and they need to be expressed. However, learning the facts involved in the whole story might change those same feelings.

    We must not make the truth of our feelings always *synonymous* with the truth of the facts. They may be quite different. Respect the feelings, but make certain of the facts! We also need to be careful that we represent truth correctly. People will sometimes misrepresent, exaggerate, or even distort a version of the truth. This may happen for a number of reasons, including:

- Self-<u>preservation</u> (I don't want to lose my "place/position.")
- Self-<u>protection</u> (I want to avoid any pain or hurt.)
- Self-<u>gratification</u> (I need affirmation, strokes.)
- Self-<u>exaltation</u> (I want to be promoted.)

    Augustine once said, "Lord, deliver me from the lust of validating myself."[29]

    Dr. Billy Graham once gave a great "truth guide" regarding

our speech. He said, "May the absent always feel safe in our presence." How would we present the "truth" in facts or feelings if the person involved were present for the conversation and not absent? How do we "represent" the absent person in our conversations about situations, conflict, disagreements, or even offenses? Do we accurately share his/her true attitudes, words, and efforts? Or do we modify to get others to defend us and our position? Do we distort the story to get them to see the "facts" as we want them to be, not necessarily as they really are?

All of these principles are part of speaking "truth." But don't forget that the Bible adds one more key word—we must speak the truth in "love."

Key Word #3 – Love!

The word "love" in Ephesians 4:15 is connected to both words preceding it. First, love is expressed when we "speak" to others, instead of ignoring them or refusing to talk to them. Second, love is also expressed when we speak the "truth" to others. God so loved the world that He "spoke" to us, and He spoke the "Truth" that the world needed to hear. Love is *how* we are to speak to others. *And* it includes what we say (truth).

Anything difficult or awkward that you might say to another person might be considered by some to be unloving. Others would say it's okay to speak…just don't speak the truth to another about a need, a fault, a failure, or an offense. Can we really be loving towards another person and not speak *truth?*

In personal relationships, it's important to have both truth and love present. Truth without love *hurts*, and love without truth *hides*. Truth without love is *painful*, but love without truth is *permissive*. They balance one another.

In Scripture, we are exhorted to…
* Walk in **Love** – Ephesians 5:2
* Walk in **Light** – Ephesians 5:8

"Light" in the Bible is knowledge, purity, and *truth!* One without the other is inadequate to build healthy relationships. In Ephesians 5:1, the Bible says we are to be followers of God. God is Truth and Love in balance! He is always lovingly truthful, and truthfully loving.

A good suggestion for improving your communication with others is to use questions. Questions don't assign motives. Questions give freedom. Questions eliminate efforts to control another person or the situation. Another helpful suggestion is to watch your choice of words. For example, avoid using the pronoun "you." For example, you will want to avoid accusatory statements that assign blame to the other person. "You make me mad when you do this…" Or "You always do something to mess things up…" Love is speaking *with* people, not at them! Watch your words.

The Context Speaks

The context of Ephesians 4:15 is also significant to this whole discussion of communication because there is an immediate context and a broader, overall context.

The broader, overall context is one word: *unity*. The immediate context is also one word: *growth*. Let's look at both.

Broader Application - Unity

In Ephesians 4:1-6, 16, Paul uses several words and phrases to capture the idea of unity. He says, "As a prisoner for the Lord, then, I urge you to live a life worthy of the calling you have received. Be completely humble and gentle; be patient, bearing with one another in love. Make every effort to keep the *unity* of the Spirit through the bond of peace. There is *one* body and *one* spirit—just as you were called to one hope when you were called. *One* Lord, *one* faith, *one* baptism. *One* God and Father of all, who is over all and through all and in all…From Him (Christ), the whole body is *joined* and held *together* by every supporting ligament, and grows and builds itself up in love, as each part does its work." Obviously, doing what Ephesians 4:15 says and "speaking the truth in love" protects against division in the Body of Christ!

Immediate Application - Maturity

Paul writes, "(Instead of) being infants tossed back and forth…and blown here and there…*speaking the truth in love*, we will in all things grow up…(into Christlikeness)."
Obviously, doing what 4:15 says and "speaking the truth in love" protects against immaturity in the Body of Christ!

The Church desperately needs unity and maturity. To have these two values, we must practice Ephesians 4:15: speaking to each other truth and love. Our communication will develop or diminish our unity and our maturity as a result.

And Then There Was...Loyalty

John Maxwell writes, "When we are debating an issue, *loyalty* means giving me your honest opinion, whether you think I'll like it or not. Disagreement, at this stage, stimulates me. But once a decision has been made, the debate ends. From that point on, *loyalty* means executing the decision as if it were your own."[30] In the next chapter, we will study what role loyalty plays in building relationships with others. What we learn in the next few pages may inspire you to increase the loyalty factor in all of your key relationships and experience the benefits.

Talking Points

Guideline #2: We must learn how to communicate, and we must learn to communicate.

1. The elements of communication are listening, hearing, feeling, respect, and sensitivity.
    Ask:
    *   Which of these is a struggle for you?
    Ask:
    *   Why do people refuse to speak to one another? (answers include Hurt, Avoidance, Pride, Revenge, Disobedience, etc.)
2. There are at least two kinds of truth: <u>Facts</u> - objective, clear, observable evidence vs. <u>Feelings</u> - subjective responses, reactions, personal perspective.
    Ask:
    *   How can you listen better for both the feelings and the facts?
3. "Speaking the truth in love is <u>what</u> I say and <u>how</u> I say it." "Truth without love <u>hurts</u>, but love without truth <u>hides</u>." "Truth without love is <u>painful</u>, but love without truth is <u>permissive</u>."
    Ask:
    *   Do you agree or disagree with the above statements? Explain.
    *   Why is it important to ask good questions when you are trying to listen to another person?
    *   How can you protect against division and immaturity in the Church by how you communicate with others?

CHAPTER 7

Guideline Three: Loyalty

We must *learn* and *live* true loyalty in the Body of Christ.

Focal Passage:
"Be devoted to one another in brotherly love." Romans 12:10

E verybody loves loyalty and everybody honors it when they see it demonstrated—whether in athletics, a marriage, a job, or a patriotic cause. However, our culture is woefully short on good examples. Frederick Reichheld wrote, "For the follower, *loyalty* means that you are appreciated not just as a cog in the wheel, or as a contribution to the bottom line, but as an individual. But this is a test most current day leaders are flunking, as fewer than half of all U.S. companies employees now consider their employer to be worthy of their *loyalty*."[31]Gregory Morris adds, "For a leader, *loyalty* means I value others, not just use them."[32]

When I was growing up, my grandmother suffered with Parkinson's disease. For 17 years, she was bedridden. In all that time, my grandfather "Pop" did not flinch once in his unswerving loyalty. Pop took care of my grandmother every step of the way, initially using hired assistance to visit her daily at home. When he could no longer do everything she needed by himself, he moved both of them into a nursing home. Life wasn't easy, but Pop was loyal.

I remember one occasion when Pop hired some roofers to replace the shingles on their home. The windows were open to the bedroom where Mammaw lay. The roofers were hard at work on that side of the house on a hot summer day. The workers started using loud profanity. Hearing this, my grandfather marched out and told them, "Hey, my wife is in this room listening to all your filthy language! If anybody's going to do any cussing around here, I'll be the one to do it. So, clean up your language or you're fired right now."

The men were very apologetic, and the profanity ceased immediately and for the rest of the job. Pop "protected" Mammaw in every way and was always *loyal* to her to the very day he found she had passed away in the night. I cherish that memory and his example of devotion.

Leaders in churches know how important loyalty is in ministry, and many Pastors have even established certain requirements and expectations, including loyalty, for every Staff member they hire. One highly respected Pastor I know had four requirements for his Ministerial Staff:

- **Positive Attitude** – being able to see how God is at work in every situation and circumstance.
- **Respectful Attitude** – showing value to every person even when they disagree with you.
- **Servant Attitude** – seeking to make others a success.
- **Loyal Attitude** – not receiving anything said against another until it has first been shared with the individual personally.

This particular Pastor was well known for mentoring literally hundreds of young ministers and seminary students, including myself. He shared invaluable insights into his ministry and leadership with us. Though loyalty really is important, so much *dis*loyalty exists today. There are broken marriages, job burnouts, forced early terminations or retirements, abandoned children, and a fragmented world full of disillusioned people who believe loyalty is never reciprocated and does not count for anything anymore. *The local church has a choice!* We can either practice what we see in *society* and *imitate* the culture or practice what we see in *Scripture*…and it can *impact* the culture.

The Call to Loyalty
The Scriptures do not use the word "loyalty" at all in the King

James translation (nor is it used in newer versions). However, the concept is very clear throughout Scripture:

- **Romans 12:10** "Be *devoted* to one another in brotherly love."

   One translation says: "show family affection" (Holman) but this is a single word in the Greek, and it is actually stronger than this translation sounds. The emphasis in the verse is on the word "devoted" not on the word "love," even though the latter usually garners one's attention.

- **John 13:34** "Love one another *as* I have loved you."

   Jesus loves us with a *loyal* love...He loves us *through* stuff. Through failures, differences, immaturity, weakness, and even sin.

- **Ephesians 4:3** KJV *"Endeavor* to keep the unity of the Spirit in the bond of peace."

   The word "endeavor" suggests effort, hard work, focus, and diligence. Unity is a *gift* of the Spirit to God's people, but it has to be "kept" or "guarded." This requires loyalty to one another. Loyalty holds us fast when a problem comes up in a person's life that could make relationships difficult...and problems *will* come up!

- **Matthew 18:15-16** "If your brother sins against you, *go...take... tell* him...!"

   Many read this passage as a negative, but it is really a positive. Who else but a brother or sister Christian would go to so much trouble, or take so many steps, to restore a relationship? It would be natural just to walk away. Disloyalty cuts people off, condemns, and abandons. On the other hand, loyalty values relationships and strives to protect and maintain them.

- **John 13:35** KJV "By this shall all men know you are my disciples, if you have love (loyalty) one for another." (parentheses added)

   A love that is loyal is a different kind of love. Being loyal to another though difficulties, differences, and disappointments is the way we are to love one another.

An Insight about Loyalty

As a Pastor, I discovered that you <u>can</u> be loyal to God's truth *and* to your Christian brother at the same time. It does not have to be one or the other. You don't have to compromise your brother for truth, or truth for your brother.

There will be tough decisions required for all churches at times, involving good people and people you love. Avoidance is not the answer. Sometimes there is a need for earnest prayer and delay, but not avoidance.

People need to prayerfully seek God's way of resolution when conflicts arise, and they need to know there *is* a way, even while remaining loyal. The world will notice if a local church practices a different level of loyalty than that to which they are accustomed.

The Clarification About Loyalty

Loyalty is often misunderstood or misrepresented, even in a church and/or ministry. No one wants to be called "disloyal" or thought of as being such, but sometimes the confusion about loyalty creates a false sense of failure in that area. A better understanding of what the term actually means will help people avoid disloyalty in the local church—and it will help them avoid false guilt. First, let's look at what loyalty is **NOT**:

- Loyalty is **not** *fear,* or fear-based actions and conformity.

  Some people, even in ministry, have been told they must "comply or else." The strong threat of being fired, along with the accusation of being guilty of "disloyalty" is forced upon them to bring about a desired action, behavior, response, support, decision, or attitude. The high value the employee has for loyalty creates tension. The employee wants to please and be perceived as loyal, but there is a struggle to be "loyal" when authenticity or genuine respect is absent. True loyalty is not fear-driven.

- Loyalty is **not** the compromise of *truth.* (e.g., God's truth, or your honest feelings and self-concept, or your true thoughts about something). Loyalty does not practice dishonesty with oneself or others.

- Loyalty is **not** the loss of personal *choice.*

- Loyalty is **not** the loss of personal *self-respect, worth,* or *dignity.*

  Think about it. God asks loyalty from each of us, but His request does not require the loss of our self-respect, worth, or dignity. To the contrary, it adds to our self-respect, worth, and dignity.

- Loyalty is **not** the sacrifice of your *integrity,* values, or beliefs.

  If a person is called upon to sacrifice these in the name of "loyalty," the issue is not loyalty at all.

Three Truths about Loyalty

Let me express some key truths about the concept of loyalty in a different way.

1. If a person is asked to forfeit truth, choice, integrity, or respect in the name of "loyalty," then the issue is really one of *control* and manipulation, whether the relationship is a marriage, a job, or a church.
2. Too many people have been made to feel disloyal in a relationship when, in fact, they have only refused to be *abused*. We need to stop the abuse, even in the Church!
3. To control how people feel, think, or choose is more *cultic* than Christian. Cults say "don't." Don't think, feel, choose for yourself, or be yourself under God. Just follow, obey, and conform. Give away your freedom, choices, and personal understanding to another. Loyalty, though, is not control.

So, what is **true** *loyalty?*

Webster's dictionary definition for loyalty is "devotion, true allegiance, being constant and faithful in any relationship."

Notice the word *devotion*, which occurs in Romans 12:10 in our focal verse for this chapter. Devotion is about a deep, enduring commitment to another's growth, personal good, and purposeful self-fulfillment. Loyalty is healthy, it's true, and it is desirable. For certain, it is required in God's family.

Here's my personal definition for loyalty: Loyalty is the *freedom* to be true to myself and to God, and then to others in my relationships as I serve them, serve with them, stand with them, or stand under them, *voluntarily*.

In this definition, loyalty is also a *gift*. It's given to those with whom we share much in common. Among Christians, we share a common:

- Cause - The common *cause* is the calling to extend God's kingdom on earth.
- Commitment - The common *commitment* is we are members of one Body by our personal choice.
- Convictions - The common *convictions* are the biblical beliefs we share.
- Connection - The common *connection* is we are spiritually kin through the blood of Jesus Christ. That is the tie that truly binds us together.

It should be natural for us to be deeply loyal to fellow members of the faith. Oh, that the local church and individual believers could capture this sense of being an *army*, a *Body*, a *team*, and a *family!* Loyalty would then flow as the free gift we would gladly give to our brothers and sisters in Christ!

The Commitment of Loyalty

Now that we understand a working definition of loyalty, let's look at the practical side of it. There are different expressions of loyalty demonstrated in the Body of Christ, but one very important beginning point concerns how we talk about one another. Our loyalty begins first with our words and our communication. Here's a good declaration in our practice of loyalty:

"I will neither *speak* nor *receive* a negative report about another person in our fellowship until I know it has first been shared with them personally and directly."

The biblical basis for this principle is Matthew 18, which instructs us to go to a person *first* before ever going to others *about* them. Every believer needs to make this commitment to God, simply because they want to be a loyal church member in the family of God.

However, what does the word "receive" mean in this example? We know what "speaking" ill about someone means, but what about "receiving" a negative report about another?

To "receive" a negative report about another is to do one or all of the following:

- To *accept* the report as truth or fact, even when it might not be (or it might not be completely true).
- To *affirm* its validity to the person reporting it, or to others, as if you know all the facts or can read people's motives.
- To take *action* based on the substance of the report (such as repeating it to others, making a decision based upon the report, or coming to a judgment). This can hurt relationships!

To not "receive" a negative report about another person in the fellowship is to remind the person sharing the report to obey Matthew 18 and to caution that person not to repeat this information.

I knew one Pastor who skillfully used this truth in a number of situations. I noted some of his responses when confronted with a "negative report" about someone else. In one case, he told the person repeating the report, "I don't need to hear that." In another he replied, "I can't receive that (accept it, affirm it, or act on it) until it has been shared with them personally. Have you done that?"

Still another Pastor I once overheard had this direct answer: "You know what the Bible says in Matthew 18. It's wrong for us to discuss this without going to that person. Are you going to do that?" Then he went on to say, "It's as much a wrong for us to violate Matthew 18 as anything that person may have done that is wrong."

What a clear practice and example of loyalty! Any Christian would greatly appreciate someone refusing to receive something said about him or her in a negative report without being approached about it first. That's love as well as loyalty. Even a believer that was guilty of the wrong that was being reported would so value that kind of loyalty shown by a fellow Christian. However, let me tell you what too often happens to relationships in the local church. One person shares a negative report to another person and it gets passed on until a group of 8-10 others all believe it and get upset. Then the person being talked about doesn't even know why the relationships around him have started to change!

There is an important exception to note. There *is* a proper time to talk with others first before going directly to the brother or sister in question, without it being an act of disloyalty. There are two cases where this is permissible, in my opinion. When you are seeking...

1. Insight to help. How should I approach this person? What words should I use? Will you pray for me as I go?
2. Involvement to help. Will you go with me? Will you be an objective observer and offer input and perspective? Will you verify our words?

The Contrast to Loyalty – Disloyalty

Disloyalty, in a word, is *disassociation*. It begins in private in a person's heart and in their feelings and thoughts toward another person. It then becomes more public and social if it is not handled properly. It is a sad scenario that plays out in many Christian circles. It goes like this. One person feels the "cold shoulder" from another. There is a distance, a separation between the two people in words, activities, and fellowship. Disloyalty then takes the form of noticeable avoidance and gossip, and finally it can become obvious opposition. The victim of such a pattern of disloyalty feels completely surprised, perhaps even betrayed, as they consider the actions of a person once thought of as a friend. So, how do we know if we have been disloyal to another believer?

When we <u>receive</u> and <u>repeat</u> negative reports.
- Instead of doing this, encourage people to give others the benefit of the doubt. Years ago, a ladies' ministry leader in a church I pastored came to me about the conflicts she was having with other leaders in that ministry. As she shared the problems, she actually said with honest conviction, "The devil is in them." Of course, I knew these other ladies well and they were equally outstanding, sincere people just like the lady talking to me. As best I could, I tried to encourage this lady to view the others as "good people" and give them every benefit of the doubt. I told her the other ladies were not perfect, but they were honest, genuine Christians who loved God and cared about others. If she would approach them, believing what I told her, they could probably easily work out their disagreements and differences of opinion. But, try as I may, the lady picked up bits and pieces of every negative report she could find and developed a "characterization" of the other ladies that was totally out of balance and largely untrue. It kept them from ever being able to work together. Eventually, this lady and her family moved from our church. There was a wall of disloyalty between this lady and her sisters in the Lord that was built upon negative reports.
- Instead of receiving a negative report, approach others expecting the best, not the worst. Don't go with your mind made up. Ask, don't accuse or attack. Seek to clarify. Good comes from good people.
- Also, don't take up offenses from negative reports against other people in the church. "Receiving" negative reports leads to polarization, division, and personal bitterness against others. Be loyal to *all!*

When we raise <u>opposition</u> against another person, or support it privately, instead of working with the person <u>first</u> for improvement or change.
- Matthew 18, James 5:19-20, and Galatians 6:1-2 all suggest working with a fellow believer who is in error, sin, or trouble. That's loyalty.

When we fail to stand with a fellow believer when he or she faces the natural <u>adversities</u> of life while serving the Lord.

- Any ministry doing *anything* significant for the glory of God will face adversity. That's a time when people need our deepest expression of loyalty and love to stand by them.

So, why do people become disloyal? What are the motives? I believe there are three common motives when it comes to practicing disloyalty. See if you hear anything familiar in the following examples of someone being disloyal:

- Self-<u>Promotion</u>: "This is my chance, my opportunity." "I have been wanting this position."
- Self-<u>Protection</u>: "I have to take care of me." "Someone else can pay a price if they want to, but I am not."
- Self-<u>Profit</u>: "I want more." "I can profit through another's demise." "I value the profit more than the relationship or the other person."

A Story about Disloyalty

Loyalty in the Church has been based far too often upon *performances* or *preferences*. Loyalty needs to begin with one thing...relationships. It needs to be based simply upon the "value" of eternity, which is people!

What do I mean by that? First, in the area of *performances* we tend to ask what people have done or not done before we'll be devoted. We require a certain performance from them before giving them our loyalty. In other words we say, "I will be loyal to you...if you do such and such. Or as long as you do what I want or think is right. Or as long as you believe and perform in a certain way." Even Pastors are sometimes granted loyalty by their membership, or loyalty is withheld, based upon their performance. This is certainly true for church Staff members as well.

Years ago in one of my pastorates, I communicated my personal conviction about weddings. I would not perform a wedding ceremony for a couple living together out of wedlock unless they separated and prepared themselves in every way for a God-honoring and God-centered marriage.

A prominent couple in my church had a granddaughter living with her boyfriend. The young couple decided to get married the next year. I was out of state at the time speaking at a Pastors retreat when the grandmother called the church office one Friday. My secretary gently shared my conviction for officiating at any wedding. (I suspect the grandmother knew this already but wanted me to change my mind for the sake of their granddaughter, who also happened to have a significant learning disability that hindered her reasoning.) The prospective groom had also made it clear he wouldn't separate before getting married. In my absence, my secretary tried to support my position by counseling the grandmother biblically. She also told the grandmother that she didn't really believe I would make an exception (which was true). The grandmother expressed her disappointments, but she was cordial and hung up the phone.

On Sunday morning, I was still absent. The grandparents and all their extended family came to church and took their usual places serving in the nursery and children's ministries. Everything seemed normal. However, at a certain pre-arranged time and without warning, they as a family left the church! They left their classes and ministries unattended. My secretary related the story to me by phone that Sunday afternoon. This was a large extended family, so their abrupt departure "sent a message." To make a long story short, this family never returned (all 20-30 of them). The good news is that our church survived and eventually thrived.

What made this experience so painful for me was that I had served as Pastor and friend to this entire family. I had visited their sick family members, preached their funerals, counseled them in crisis, etc. I thought they would always be loyal to me! How wrong I was. When my "performance" did not suit them, they couldn't serve with me (much less under me) any more. Their loyalty to me was not based on me as a person or Pastor, or even a principle—it was solely based upon my performance, according to their expectations.

A Higher Level

The Church needs a higher level of loyalty. We need to be loyal to people as family and committed to each other even when we disagree with someone's performance. That does not mean we don't confront sin or practice church discipline, as needed. In fact, I'll address that topic a little later in this book. However, it does mean that we are loyal to people, even while taking the biblical steps of confrontation, correction, or discipline that may be required. In fact, as we will see later, biblical church discipline when practiced correctly is one of the highest forms of loyalty that we in the Body of Christ can demonstrate.

In the matter of "preferences," too often our loyalty is negatively affected by our differences. Think of the "worship wars" in so many churches. Can you imagine the two words "worship" and "wars" even being placed together in the same sentence? Terrible things have been done and said in churches because loyalty was not based on people but upon preferences.

It's time we emphasized that *relationships* in the local church are a priority. It's time for us to be loyal to one another as God's people and family, above our personal performances and preferences! Look at the following very simple diagram:

Us ➡ Bad Performances/Different Preferences ➡ Disloyalty!
God ➡ Persons with Bad Performances / Diverse Preferences ➡ Loyalty Still!

"God says 'I will *never* leave you nor forsake you…Come now, though your sins be as scarlet…Being confident of this one thing, that He who has begun a good work in you will perform it until the day of Jesus Christ'" (Hebrews 13:5, Isaiah 1:18, Philippians 1:6).

What about God and our relationship with Him? Scripture is clear. Performance and preference never affect His loyalty to us! He never leaves us or walks out on us. He never distances Himself from us or stops being true to us. Forever, He loves us and works to redeem us.

So, what's the application? Christians are to be like Him in their relationships with each other! If we are going to be disloyal to anyone, let it be to the devil! And let believers disassociate with *him* and all *his* ways! You see, loyalty is already a "big deal" in the family, the workplace, in sports and in our military service. Likewise, Christians need to make it a "big deal" in the local church, learning the truth about what it really is so they can live it out in their spiritual relationships!

Talking Points

Guideline #3: We must learn and live out true loyalty.

1. You don't have to compromise your brother for truth, or truth for your brother.
   Ask:
   - How can you be loyal to God's truth and to your brother at the same time?
2. Many people have confused loyalty with control. Read over the list below and share a personal example of how you learned this truth:
   - Loyalty is not fear, or fear-based actions.
   - Loyalty is not the compromise of truth. (Feelings, Self, Thoughts, God's)
   - Loyalty is not the loss of choice.
   - Loyalty is not the loss of personal self-respect, worth, or dignity.
   - Loyalty is not the sacrifice of your integrity, values, or beliefs.
3. The Commitment of Loyalty: "I will neither speak nor receive a negative report about another person in our fellowship until I know it has first been shared with them personally and directly."
   Ask:
   - In what ways are negative reports dangerous in the Church?
4. The motives behind disloyalty are:
   1. Self-Promotion 2. Self-Protection 3. Self-Profit
   Ask:
   - In what ways have you seen disloyal motivations at work in the Church?
5. "Loyalty in the Church has been based far too much upon performances or preferences. It needs to begin with one thing…relationships, and be based upon people."
   Ask:
   - How can we be loyal to people without regard to their performance/preferences?

CHAPTER 8

Guideline Four: Caring Confrontation

We must *care* enough to *confront* sin or error, in belief or behavior in the family of faith.

Focal Passage:
"My <u>brothers</u>, if one of you should <u>wander</u> (err) from the truth, and someone should <u>bring you back</u> (convert); remember this: Whoever turns (converts) a <u>sinner</u> away from his error will save him from <u>death</u>, and <u>cover</u> (hide) a multitude of sins."(KJV in parentheses)
James 5:19-20

Confrontation is never fun. John Ortberg tells the story about a Pastor who needed to confront an individual who was causing conflict in the church. But the reluctant Pastor confided to his wife that he was afraid to speak to the troublemaker because "every time I think about this person, I get sweaty palms and every time I have to confront someone, my mouth goes dry." His wife simply responded, "Why don't you just lick your palms?"[33]

John Maxwell in his book, *Developing the Leader Within*

You, offers a suggestion for those who struggle and feel uneasy with the word "confront" itself. He uses the word "clarify," making the distinction between clarifying an issue instead of confronting a person. In the same book, he also gives what he calls, "The Ten Commandments of Confrontation."[34] He covers the important basics of confronting someone privately (not publicly), being specific with your words and avoiding sarcasm and generalities. When confronting another, it's about winning, not losing; restoration, not rejection. It's about building up, not tearing down. We must care enough to confront sin or error, in belief or behavior, with the members of our family of faith. This is an imperative truth in many scriptures throughout both the Old and New Testaments. Healthy relationships require dependable, loving, and faithful accountability.

Deitrich Bonhoeffer, the esteemed German Pastor who died at the hands of the Nazis shortly before the end of WWII, once wrote these words, "He who no longer listens to his brother, will soon no longer be listening to God."

We all need our brothers and sisters to speak into our lives, not as a judge or Pharisee, but as a loyal and caring family member. Perhaps the greatest prerequisite for being properly prepared to speak into the life of another is being willing and ready to have others speak into one's own life first. If we are not ready to "receive" correction, we may not be ready to "give" it.

Cain's question at the beginning of human history in Genesis 4:9 speaks to our mutual responsibility. He asked God, "Am I my brother's keeper?" Bottom line, Cain was actually trying to excuse himself from any responsibility or accountability for his brother, as well as for his own guilt for his murderous act. He was saying, "I am not responsible for him, and I am not responsible for what has happened to him." Do you see the picture? Having no responsibility in a relationship for a person's whereabouts or direction is dangerous (spiritually as well as physically). Having no responsibility for my actions toward another person is equally destructive.

What was God's answer to Cain's questions? Consider the following New Testament passages:

- Romans 14:7 "For none of us lives to himself alone, and none of us dies to himself alone."

In other words, no man is an island in the Body of Christ.

There are no "Lone Rangers" or "one-man bands." We are inter-connected in our influences and in our choices, due to our relationships with one another.

- 1 Corinthians 6:19-20 "You are not your own...glorify God..."
    The believer is not alone, and not his/her own. There is no independence from God or from His purposes with people.
- 1 Corinthians 12:12-26 "The body is a unit, though it is made up of many parts..."
    We belong to God *and* to one another because we are one "Body."

Willing to Take a Risk

Is caring confrontation difficult and even risky? Sure it is. A little boy was once asked to give a brief essay on Socrates. He got up before his class and made four pointed statements:

"Socrates was a Greek. Socrates was a great man. Socrates told people how to live their lives. They *poisoned* Socrates."

The risk we take is real. The pain and hurt can be deep and significant. But anything worthwhile usually has its costs or possible risks, and people and relationships are definitely worthwhile and valuable.

Two preliminary cautions are important. First, believers don't need to "address" every single sin in a brother or sister's life. The ones that really matter are the ongoing ones hurting relationships or a church's ministry and testimony. Second, the idea behind confrontation is always to help and support one another, not to hurt or to hinder. It's not telling people how to live their lives. Perspective and preparation are essential, along with prayer.

Confronting Biblically

Let's go back to our focal passage from James: "My <u>brothers</u>, if one of you should <u>wander</u> (err) from the truth, and someone should <u>bring you back</u> (convert); remember this: Whoever turns (converts) a <u>sinner</u> away from his error will save him from <u>death</u>, and <u>cover</u> (hide) a multitude of sins." James 5:19-20 (KJV in parentheses)

Notice the key words marked in this passage and the understanding gained from two translations of the same scripture.

- "Brothers" – the passage is written *to* Christians and *about* Christians

This is a "Church Family" context. This ministry is for Christians, with Christians.

- "Wander from the truth" – in *behavior* or *beliefs*

  One usually leads to the other. People who believe the wrong things will behave wrongly. People who behave wrongly will either change their behavior to accommodate their beliefs or change their beliefs to accommodate their behavior. They won't live with conviction or guilt. Notice, too, that a Christian *can* err from the truth, which includes Pastors, Deacons, Teachers, and Leaders. We are all *forgiven* of our sin, but we are never *free* from it completely in this life.

- "Someone" – a Christian is God's *missionary* to another Christian.

  God's *provision* for a sinning brother is not an angel, a lightning bolt, or a voice from heaven that sounds like thunder. It is a *fellow* believer—it's us! It is a Christian who loves and cares for "family."

- "Bring you back" – NIV

  The NASV renders this "turn him back." The KJV uses the word "convert." When Christians use the word "convert," we usually think of converting the lost for salvation. Here the idea would be converting the saved (sanctification).

  This "conversion" is about our walk in Christ, not our life in Christ. There will be believers in every local Body who need to experience this type of conversion. Sometimes it is more difficult to "convert" the saved than it is the lost!

- "Death" – In this passage, death is not an eternal consequence but an earthly one. There are different forms of "death" believers can experience including death to opportunities, to relationships, to blessings, to health, to influence, to power, to their witness, to resources, and then physical death itself. Sin always brings forth death. (James 1:15)

  God uses "family members" to turn/bring "family members" back, in love and in truth, not in judgment or condemnation. This is a ministry *of* the Church *to* the Church. This ministry responsibility given to all Christians (not just Pastors, Staff, Deacons or Elders) is literally a matter of life and death (and not just physical death)!

- "Cover" – The idea is not *concealment* but *covering*.

  Concealment means our attempt at not being found out

or exposed. Covering is forgiveness and the limitation of sin's consequences. The consequences are halted or held up.

- "Multitude" – Sin always begets sin. When King David started down the road to his great spiritual debacle, his first sin was lust. Then lust produced adultery, adultery produced deception, deception led to dishonesty, and finally murder and hypocrisy came into his life. Each sin adds to the damage and hammers another nail into the coffin of death for a believer.

It can be said that Christ's work is redemption, and the Christian's work is reclamation. God sent His Son to redeem us. God sends His saints to reclaim and restore us. God so loves His people that He never lets them go!

Caring Enough to Confront

How can Christians "convert" Christians when necessary if they don't care enough to confront? The answer is they can't. Proverbs 27:5 says, "Open rebuke is better than secret love." (KJV) The NIV renders this same verse: "Better is open rebuke than hidden love." Failure to confront a brother or sister is actually love withheld. The word "secret" in Proverbs 27:5 means "withdrawn."

What is the method of confrontation described in the Bible? Jesus taught us in Matthew 18:15-17:

"If your brother sins against you, go and show him his fault, just between the two of you. If he listens to you, you have won your brother over. But if he will not listen, take one or two others along, so that 'every matter may be established by the testimony of two or three witnesses.' If he refuses to listen to them, tell it to the church; and if he refuses to listen even to the church, treat him as you would a pagan or a tax collector."

Let's break it down into a sequence of steps.
1. <u>Procedure</u> – Alone first, then with another or others as needed and helpful.
2. <u>Purpose</u> – To help, not hurt; assist, not accuse; restore, not reject or ruin.
3. <u>Prayer</u> – God's will done God's way = God's work.
   Chuck Swindoll once suggested the possibility that it is possible to move someone's heart by prayer alone. It is *with*

prayer, *in* prayer, *after* prayer, and *always* prayer.

4. <u>Perspective</u> – Family, not foes.
5. <u>Purity</u> – God demands, desires, and blesses holiness. Holiness is not perfection but progress towards godliness in Christian living and character. (1 Peter 1:15-16)

Restoring a Christian Brother or Sister

Christians have a clear mandate to restore the fallen. If Christians or a local church do not fulfill this mandate, they are irresponsible, and they forfeit their credibility before the unbelieving world. To preach against sin, or vote against sin, and then do nothing about sin in our midst is hypocritical. "The world watches, then holds us accountable to what we preach, when we don't." (Anonymous) Galatians 6:1 has some insights for us on this subject. "Brothers, if someone is <u>caught</u> (overtaken) in a <u>sin</u> (fault), you who are spiritual <u>should</u> restore him gently." (KJV)

- "Caught" – trapped by the sin, not exposed before people.
- "Spiritual" – not positions or knowledge, but experienced and mature. A person   walking with God, bearing the continual fruit of the Spirit. (Galatians 5:22-23)
- "Restore" – setting broken bones, to mend.

    This word reminds us it is a positive ministry of help and assistance. It is not negative or destructive and damaging. A spiritual believer becomes like a "physician's assistant" to the Great Physician in restoration and healing.
- "Gently" – carefully, with compassion.

    Restoration is a ministry of the heart, not just the hands. It is not done in a rough or reckless manner. Otherwise, it is not Christlike. Christ surely does not deal with us in such a manner.

In Ken Blanchard's book, *Leading at a Higher Level,* he addresses the subject of confrontation using the word "reprimand" and gives some excellent insights from the business world. For example, he writes that a reprimand is appropriate only for someone who has the skills to do a job, but for some reason or attitude, chooses not to do so. Blanchard's suggestions include being expedient with a reprimand as soon as possible after the offense. He also suggests having an honest conversation that targets a specific incident or offense, not mere generalities. Like many authors, he emphasizes reaffirming and encouraging the person after the confrontation, too.[35] According to Webster's dictionary, the word *affirm* comes from *ad firmore*, which means "to make firm."

Discipline in the Church
So, how does this play out in the real world? In the next two chapters, I outline a very practical method for discipline and restoration that we actually used in one of my former churches.

Talking Points

Guideline #4: We must care enough to confront sin or error, in belief or behavior, with the members of our family of faith.

1. "A Christian is God's missionary to another Christian."
   Ask:
   - Do you agree with the above statement? Explain.
   - According to the Bible, we belong to each other in the Body of Christ—why is this important?

2. Sin always brings death. (James 1:5)
   Ask:
   - In what ways does sin bring a form of "death"? (Answers include: Walk with God, Opportunities, Usefulness, Growth, Relationships, Blessings, Health, Resources, Witness, Influence, Power, Physical, etc.)
   - Why is the ministry of reconciliation a matter of life and death?

3. God sent His Son to redeem us! God sent His Saints to reclaim us!
   Ask:
   - How can Christians "convert" Christians if they don't care enough to confront?
   - How would you summarize the process of reconciliation in Matthew 18?

4. A spiritual believer becomes like a physician's assistant to the Great Physician in restoration and healing. Restoration is a ministry of the heart, not just the hands.
   Ask:
   - When was a time God used you to spiritually restore/heal another person? What did you learn?

CHAPTER 9

Church Discipline and Restoration

E very church needs to establish some fundamental principles for church discipline based on biblical guidelines. Overlooked disobedience and impurity are damaging in the Body of Christ. The Bible says in 1 Corinthians 5:6, "a little leaven leavens the whole lump of dough." If a church fails to address the flagrant disobedience of one member, others may take their own sin less seriously, too. Church discipline has a purpose beyond dealing with sin itself—it must go hand in hand with an effort toward restoration and growth, which is always the overall goal.

The American Church is unholy and undistinguishable from society today. It's not just a problem of preaching the wrong message but also a failure to implement it into people's lives. The reality is that we don't appear to care how people behave, as long as they believe the right things. To preach the truth and not practice it in the Church is hypocritical, just as it is in one's personal life. The Bible makes it clear that the Church is to expect a biblical standard of holiness among its members (see Acts 5, 1 Corinthians 5, 2 Thessalonians 3).

The issue of church discipline and restoration is not necessarily a popular topic, but it is a necessary one. Pastors from a previous generation stressed it from the pulpit much more than it seems to be talked about today. Pastor John J.

Dagg, a pastor in the 1800s and former President of Mercer University, once observed in his Manual of Church Order, "When discipline leaves the church, Christ goes with it." What a sobering thought for us to consider if we neglect this key issue. Hezekiah Harvey, a professor of theology from Madison University in the late 1800s, went so far as to say disobedience in the church "paralyzes the power of the pulpit." He adds, "...no other cause, probably, is so potent for evil in the churches as the general neglect of a true church discipline" (from *The Church: Its Policy and Ordinances*).

However, don't think of church discipline as merely a negative. It actually benefits the church in many ways. Patrick Mell, former President of the Southern Baptist Convention in the late 1800s, also noted the positive aspects in his work, *Corrective Church Discipline*. He describes it as a built-in protection for the church's reputation that both warns the church members and ultimately blesses the offender.

The issue, therefore, is a serious one. I join with today's modern voices still calling for churches to pay attention to disobedience among their members or lose their witness in the world. When we refuse to deal with sin in the church, "it eases the rebuke of a lost world that is alienated from God and in need of the Gospel," wrote J. W. MacGorman, Distinguished Professor of New Testament at Southwestern Seminary, in his book, *The People of God.*[36]

However, many churches today may not know why, when, or how to implement the process of church discipline. When I served at Northway Baptist Church in Angleton, I researched and gathered materials on church discipline from some of the greatest churches and theologians in America, past and present. A very capable attorney in our church then did a masterful job of writing a biblical guide for one section in Northway's church constitution.

For the purposes of this book, I have pulled from that original material for Northway and provided additional editorial revisions and suggestions. Although I encourage you to tailor your guidelines based on your own study of Scripture, this is a good start that can help guide any church through the toughest confrontations. What I wrote at the introduction of this material for Northway captures the reason why I feel this matter is important for churches:

RELATIONSHIP KEEPERS

If we are going to have a responsible church membership, and if church membership itself is going to really mean anything at Northway in the future, we must learn to practice the ministry of discipline and restoration among ourselves in a consistent, healthy, loving and biblical manner.
— Kent Pate, July 21, 2002

Discipline and Restoration

The pivotal issue of church discipline and restoration is the responsibility of a church to speak the Word of God to its members and to keep watch over their souls. (Hebrews 13:7) This same passage tells us that church leadership will give an account for such watch care. Therefore, it is essential that we understand the various biblical components.

The Place of Discipline and Restoration

The place of discipline and restoration is the Church. All church discipline is to occur within a church—the assembled community of redeemed, believing people. It is a "family matter" and not the responsibility of a certain committee. It is "one another oriented" (horizontal) and not just "leadership-only oriented" (vertical).

The Purpose of Discipline

The primary purpose of church discipline is restoration. The purpose of church discipline is not and never will be punishment. Discipline does not exist for its own sake but instead as a tool for the Church Family to use with love and discernment. Its purpose is to bring about the restoration of a sinning brother or sister.
Of course, there are other purposes for church discipline as well. Consider the following list:

- To mature a Body of believers. *Ephesians 4:12-16; 1 Corinthians 3:1*
- To prove that the leaders love and care. *2 Corinthians 7:12*
- To intensify self-examination in the Church. *2 Corinthians 7:11*
- To affirm obedience to God's authority. *2 Corinthians 2:9*
- To purify the spirit and message of the Church. *1 Corinthians 5:6*
- To destroy fleshly lusts in a believer. *1 Corinthians 5:5*
- To confirm individual responsibility for one another. *Hebrews 3:13*
- To deny Satan any advantage in the Church. *2 Corinthians 2:11*
- To protect scripture from perversion and error. *Titus 1:10-11*

- To cut emotional ties with unrepentant Christians.
  1 Corinthians 5:11

The Person of Discipline and Restoration
Initially, the person of discipline is the *offended* brother (Matthew 18:15) and not some committee nor church leadership. In most cases, addressing the individual is all that will be needed to correct the situation. It is the responsibility of every member in the Body who is "spiritual" (Galatians 6:1), that is, believers who walk in the Spirit (Galatians 5:16) and are mature in the faith (1 Corinthians 2:15; Hebrews 5:13-14) to address the sin that they see. The purity of the Body is every believer's concern. This will require, on occasion, more than simply a prayer of wishful thinking and may often require loving confrontation. This responsibility of every individual to lovingly confront can be neither sidestepped nor delegated.

The Provocation of Discipline and Restoration
The provocation of discipline is "if your brother sins against you." (Matthew 18:15) The types of sin are not listed, as all sin must be addressed. If the Body of believers is working properly, most individuals will be dealing with their own sin. From time to time, however, it will become necessary for members to lovingly confront other members. All sin is against another believer, either directly or indirectly, and must be addressed and confronted in love.

The Prerequisites of Discipline and Restoration
The prerequisites of discipline and restoration are crucial. Before taking the first step in the process of going to the fellow believer, there are certain steps that must be taken.

Examine Self – When one becomes aware of a sinning believer (and even before the initial step of going to him in private), you must "first take the log out of your own eye, and then you will see clearly to take the speck out of your brother's eye." (Matthew 7:5) Doing so will require you to first examine yourself to see if there is any sinful motivation for wanting to confront someone. The driving force behind your confrontation must be a fellow believer's good. The only reason to address the speck in my brother's eye is to benefit him, not me.

Examine the Root of Disobedience – The second issue to cover before beginning the process of discipline or restoration

RELATIONSHIP KEEPERS

is an assessment of the root of the rebellion. First Thessalonians 5:14 identifies three different reasons why a brother might stray from the truth, and each reason requires a different response. *"...Admonish the unruly, encourage the faint hearted, help the weak."* Before confronting a sinning brother, we must determine whether he is unruly, faint-hearted, or weak.

The word "unruly" connotes the idea of being "out of line." It is a picture of someone who strays from the prescribed life of Scripture. Such a brother is to be continually and firmly admonished (present imperative).

The "faint hearted" can be described as timid, discouraged, or frightened, or one who does not know what to do. The faint hearted does not need admonishing but instead needs encouraging, perhaps with additional instructions.

One who is "weak" is without power or one who knows what to do but is unable to do it. These have not yet learned to lean on the Lord as much as they should for their spiritual needs. One who is weak needs help or support.

In order to determine which one of these three conditions is at the root of the problem, first ask God for wisdom and insight. Second, err on the side of believing the best and approach them as if they are weak or faint-hearted, expecting to find a teachable, repentant heart. If, however, they are unruly, that will become evident by their response.

The Process of Discipline and Restoration
The four-step process for discipline and restoration is clear in Matthew 18. It's such an important process that I only want to cover the first two steps in this chapter. We'll look at the last two steps of this process in the next chapter.

Step 1: Tell Him His Sin Alone
You are ready to take Step 1 once you have examined your own heart and taken it to the Lord. Once you have looked at what might be behind their erring, you are then to "go and reprove him in private." (Matthew 18:15) This literally means speaking "between you and him alone." If you speak of the matter to anyone else before him or beside him, then you have sinned. If he listens to you, you have won your brother. If he is unrepentant, you must move to Step 2, which we will cover in a minute.

Step 1 can take place in two forms. First, the sinning believer is contacted by a mature believer strictly based on Matthew 18:15. If the sinning believer repents, praise the Lord! No contact with church leadership is necessary.

However, for another example, let's say that the leadership of a local church is approached by a brother or sister in the Lord for the purpose of informing them about a sinning believer's behavior...but he or she has not yet personally gone to the sinning believer, as Scripture requires. It is then the leadership's responsibility to follow up. I suggest the following procedure, based on what we used at Northway:

- Lovingly instruct the approaching brother or sister concerning the biblical restoration process. Have them read Matthew 18 and give them specific assistance relative to the prerequisites of discipline we covered earlier.
- Since the approaching mature believer has brought the issue to the church, it now becomes the church leadership's responsibility to expect the mature believer to initiate reconciliation by a certain date. If the meeting does not take place, the church leadership needs to determine why it has not and proceed to work toward making this happen. It is possible, based on the seriousness of the charge and knowledge of the situation, for Step 1 to be carried out by a now-informed member of the church leadership.

If the church leadership is repeatedly unable to contact the mature believer to find out if Step 1 has taken place, the church leadership will have to contact the sinning believer. You might say something like: "_____ (mature believer) indicated to me that they were going to contact you on a very sensitive matter. Have they done so?" Clarify where needed and prayerfully proceed to setting up a meeting and proceed with Step 1.

Step 2: Take Some Witnesses

"But if he does not listen to you, take one or two more with you, so that by the mouth of two or three witnesses every fact may be confirmed." (Matthew 18:16) Several issues must be clarified with this step. There is no indication that it is a matter for the Deacons, Elders, or Staff at this point, but it may be wise to involve a Deacon, Elder, Staff member, or trusted representative of either group.

Paul indicates that the only criteria for witnesses are "you who are spiritual"—that is, any Spirit-filled believer. (Galatians 6:1) James simply relegated the responsibility to "brethren." (James 5:19-20)

Logically, it is not a requirement that they serve as witnesses to the sin. Rather, they are there to bear witness to the fact of this brother's unwillingness to repent. The focus of discipline is no longer the symptom (immorality, drinking, stealing, etc.). Now the focus shifts to the root sin (rebellion, a lack of repentance, etc.).

Why are witnesses taken? *So that every fact may be confirmed.* God established this procedure in Deuteronomy 19:15 to prevent the passing on of unconfirmed, slanderous information. The witnesses are for the protection of the one being approached, as well as those making the approach. They support a consensus of both what is said and the response. The witnesses are also there to enlarge and extend the appeal.

If there is repentance, then counseling and appropriate accountability should be considered. If repentance is not apparent at this point, contact with the church leadership (e.g., Elders, Deacons, Pastors) should follow. The church leadership should contact the sinning believer and appeal for a prayerful change and response. They should also inform the sinning believer that the matter will be brought before the Deacon or Elder Body as a whole by a certain date.

If repentance is *still* not apparent following contact by the church leadership within the time frame specified, then the matter is to be brought before the Deacon or Elder Body. They will then contact the sinning believer as a Body and appeal for a prayerful change and response. At the same time, this is their opportunity to notify the sinning believer that the rights and privileges of church membership will be suspended. Further, the Deacon or Elder Body should inform the sinning believer that the matter will have to be brought before the church Body as a whole by a certain date, unless repentance is apparent. When the church is informed in Step 3, the church should then be encouraged to pray for the sinning believer and to urge repentance and reconciliation. As an example of this Step 2, see 2 Corinthians 13:1-2.

As you can see, the process is lengthy and time-intensive, but people do matter and are worth our prayerful efforts. It is never easy dealing with sin in the Church Family when you attempt to follow Christ's commands. The Bible requires us to patiently give every opportunity for restoration if possible. The next chapter reveals Steps 3 and 4 in the process and deals with the fall out of what happens when all the attempts to reconcile fail.

CHAPTER 10

Tell the Church

Step 3 involves going to the church as a whole. This is a very bold move to make—and one that has the potential to get someone's attention in a hurry. The unrepentant believer is to be notified in advance when his/her name will be brought before the church. However, this step is never used for the purpose of public shame or excommunication. The notice will give a reasonable time within which the believer may repent. The focus needs to remain the restoration of the sinning believer.

The Process of Discipline and Restoration Continued

Step 3 – Tell the Church

Jesus makes it clear that the overall aim is for the believer to "listen to the church." *"And if he refuses to listen to them (the two or three witnesses), tell it to the church."* (Matthew 18:17) The rebellion of unrepentance is to be identified as the central problem and not the initial sin, whatever it may be. If the efforts of the entire church are unable to secure the believer's repentance within an appointed time period, then the church must move to Step 4.

In a non-dramatic and yet serious manner during a church service, a representative of the Deacons, Elders, or the Senior Pastor, shares the sinning believer's name with the membership present. Enough of the details should be shared to communicate the seriousness of the situation and to also curtail unnecessary private discussion and speculation. The purpose of this step is to enlist the prayer of the church Body as well as their involvement, as the Lord leads, in calling the individual to repentance.

Church leadership then notifies the sinning believer regarding what has happened and what will happen in Step 4, if repentance is not seen. The sinning believer should also be informed of what will happen if he is repentant. For example, counseling and accountability will be instituted and the congregation made aware of the joyful news.

Step 4: Treat Him as an Outsider
"And if he refuses to listen even to the church, let him be to you as a Gentile and a tax-gatherer." (Matthew 18:17) When a member chooses to live in disregard of the covenant relationship that is the basis for membership in the Body (or no longer cares to abide by its provisions) the final step takes place. After pursuing the proper procedures for discipline and restoration, the church may remove that member's name from the membership roll. It is understood that such an action on the part of the church is taken with regret and in response to a choice made by a member to not continue in the grace relationship of church covenant membership.

In Matthew 18:17, Jesus says to treat him as an unbeliever. A church should not ignore him, nor ridicule him, but they will not fellowship with him. All further contact with him will be aimed at ministering and drawing him into fellowship with God. (2 Thessalonians 3:6; 14-15) It is important that the church leadership notify the sinning believer of the action taken. If there is still no repentance, then in similar manner as in Step 3, share with the congregation at the next church service, the heart of the action taken in this Step 4. If there is finally repentance, then share this news with the congregation at the next church service with quiet and thankful rejoicing.

The Power of Discipline and Restoration
"Whatsoever ye shall bind on earth shall be bound in heaven and whatsoever ye shall loose on earth shall be loosed in heaven." (Matthew 18:18) The power of discipline is that the church is acting in concert with God in terms of "binding" or "loosening" from sin. If you are a sinning person in a church and somebody goes to you and you do not repent, and two or three go to you and you do not repent, and the whole church is pursuing you and you

do not repent, your sins are "bound" on you. That is what God has already determined.

However, if you are in sin and you eventually repent with a broken heart, your sins are loosed and you are welcomed into the fullness of fellowship with God. Thus the Church is simply doing on earth what has already been done in heaven.

A Church That C.A.R.E.S.

Here is a simple acrostic that summarizes the steps in an easy-to-follow process. A church that practices discipline is a church that "cares" enough to do something about it, according to Scripture.

Confronts. "If thy brother trespass against thee, go and tell him his fault between thee and him alone." (Matthew 18:15, KJV) *Go* is in the present imperative and implies that you should go and pursue your "brother" without being distracted. *Tell* (Greek: elengcho) means "to expose to the light." In other words, confront the person, exposing the sin so he is aware of it and understands there is no escaping it.

Admonishes. "Yet count him not as an enemy, but admonish him as a brother." (2 Thessalonians 3:15) The word "admonish" means to verbally warn or rebuke. The admonishment is done brother to brother with a love that comes from kinship and a relationship through Jesus Christ. Again, it is not enough to just expose the sin; there must also be a challenge to repent of the sin and make restitution.

Remembers. "Brethren, if a man be overtaken in a fault, ye who are spiritual restore such an one in the spirit of meekness, considering thyself, lest thou also be tempted." (Galatians 6:1 KJV) *Considering* (Greek: skopeo) means "to heed" or "to look" with the idea of watching something closely because of possible danger. In other words, when confronting a believer, be on guard that sin (even the very same sin of your brother) is not present and unconfessed in your own life. Humility calls for a recognition that you are just as capable of sinning as your brother is.

Encourages. "Ye who are spiritual *restore* such an one." (Galatians 6:1 KJV) "Restore" (Greek: katanitzo) speaks of repairing something in the sense of bringing it back to its former condition. The word was used in secular language to set a broken bone, to mend broken nets, and to meditate and reconcile two arguing factions.

$\underline{S}$ucceeds. "He that coverteh his sins shall not prosper; but whosoever confesseth and forsaketh them shall have mercy." (Proverbs 28:13 KJV) No church discipline process is perfect or without room for adjustment, development, and wise individual application. The example I've shared in these pages worked for us at Northway. Even if the person never repents, a church is still successful if it adheres to what Scripture commands—taking every opportunity to hope for repentance.

What If the Sinning Believer Repents?

Ideally, the confrontation process reaches the final stage of discipline and then results in the repentance and restoration of a believer (which is the ultimate goal). Then what? The following is a sample of a personal confession/restoration service I used before a Church Family when this very scenario took place. I share it in hopes that you may use it as a guide for your own church.

A Personal Confession Service Before the Church Family

Opening Comments (Pastor): Tonight, we have a "family matter" we need to share together. When a family needs to talk about something, a family comes together, and that's why we have brought us all together tonight. We have some family members who need to ask for forgiveness from this Church Family. When any of us commits a sin that becomes a public reproach to the Name of Christ, to the Work of Christ, to the "name" of this Church Family or its work and ministry to others outside this Body, or to ministry to our own members, then we need to ask forgiveness of the Lord. We also need to ask forgiveness of those directly involved, and of our church (our "spiritual" family).

We want to be right with the Lord, with ourselves, with others, and with our Church Family. (Acts 24:16) In order to do that, we repent of our sin (turn away from it, have nothing to do with it), and we confess it to God and to others (1 John 1:9 and James 5:16).

I want to stress how much we are a family. God's Word says it repeatedly, but I want to revisit some of those verses that we know already. Because we are family, and because we have a relationship with others, when we sin of a public nature especially, we hurt others and not just ourselves (Romans 14:7). The relationships are *that* real and *that* strong. If we weren't family, we wouldn't need to come to one another. However, we are family, so we need to do so!

It takes a lot of courage to do this, and a lot of humility, and I am so blessed and challenged by those who are willing to participate tonight! Let me share some scriptures now for us to keep in remembrance tonight…(Pastor should comment briefly or stress key thoughts, as he is led, on the following scriptures.)

- 1 John 1:9 "If we confess our sins, God is faithful and just to forgive us our sins, and cleanse us of all unrighteousness." Forgiveness begins with our relationship with God. Believers need cleansing.
- Proverbs 28:13 "He that covers his sins shall not prosper, but whoever confesses and forsakes them shall have mercy." Part of the "forsaking" process is what we are doing tonight. We are forsaking even the compromise and covering of sin. Lots of ways exist to "cover" our sins, even in church. We do this when we ignore or overlook it. We do it when we blame others, justify, compare ourselves to others, or even increase our religious activity.
- Isaiah 1:18 "Come now, and let us reason together, says the Lord: though your sins be as scarlet, they shall be as white as snow; though they be red like crimson, they shall be as white as wool." God is a forgiving God! He calls us to His forgiveness!
- Psalm 103:2, 3, 8, 11-14 KJV "Bless the Lord, O my soul, and forget not all His benefits…who forgives all your iniquities… the Lord is merciful and gracious, slow to anger and plenteous in mercy…For as high as the heavens are above the earth, so great is His mercy toward those who fear (respect/reverence) Him… as far as the east is from the west, so far hath He removed our transgressions from us…as a father pitieth his children, so the Lord has pity for those that fear Him…For He knows our frame, and He remembers that we are but dust." If this is what the Lord is like, this is what we are supposed to be like, too, as His children!
- Hebrews 8:12 "For I will be merciful to their unrighteousness, and their sins and iniquities will I remember no more." To "remember" is to "hold against" in words, attitudes, or actions.

    <u>Pastor</u> (Specifically to the Church Family): Now to our Church Family in particular, I want to share these additional verses… (parentheses added)

- 1 Corinthians 12:26 "When one member of the body <u>hurts</u> (by sin, by consequences, etc.), <u>all</u> the members of the body hurt; when one member of the body is honored (by forgiveness, restoration, testimony), all rejoice with it."

- Galatians 6:1-2 "Brothers, if a brother or sister is overtaken (not caught, meaning exposure) in a fault or sin (and we can all get overtaken but for the grace of God), restore such a one (that is what we are doing here tonight, make no mistake…restoring one of our family back to full fellowship and acceptance in the family)…in a spirit of meekness, considering yourself also, lest you be tempted." This is to warn, humble, and help us all!
- "Bear each other's burdens (lift up), and so fulfill the Law of Christ, (which is the Law of Love)."
- James 5:16 "Confess your faults (sins, failures) to one another, and pray for one another (tonight and in the days to come) that you may be healed (healing is not just physical, but healing in the heart and life, and in relationships)."
- Ephesians 4:32 "And be kind to one another, tenderhearted (not judgmental, critical, or condemning), *forgiving one another,* even as God for Christ's sake has forgiven you!" The Forgiven are to be Forgivers! We are perhaps never so like God as when we forgive.
- Matthew 5:7 "Blessed are the merciful, for they shall obtain mercy." Mercy is not giving another person what they might deserve. We show mercy by being understanding, without being compromising.
- Matthew 6:12, 14 "Forgive us our trespasses, as we forgive those who have trespassed against us…for if you forgive men their trespasses, your Heavenly Father will also forgive you." We have no option but to forgive! Let this time of failure also cause us to check our own hearts/lives for sin, and seek individual cleansing!

Pastor asks the Sinning Brother/Sister to come forward and share with the Congregation
Some guidelines to follow for their talk:
- Be simple – no explanations or justification
- Be general – no details
- Be sincere – admit wrong and responsibility; ask for forgiveness verbally

Pastor (Standing beside the brother/sister): "Thank you for being courageous, bold, honest, genuine, humble, and obedient! As your Pastor, I forgive you completely! Church Family, if you too forgive this person completely, would you express it to them right now? (Applause, etc.)

<u>Pastor to the Person</u>: What this means tonight is you are loved, fully accepted, fully restored, and forgiven!

(Pastor asks the Person(s) to be seated.)

<u>Pastor</u> (To All): Is this important? Yes! Why? Because sin is serious! And Satan not only wants to use sin to defeat us but to divide us! We need God, and we need each other, too! Hopefully, all of us will be encouraged/warned/and strengthened tonight not to take sin for granted, or take it lightly.

This is also very important tonight because the consequences of sin are serious…

- Self Condemnation
- Broken Relationships
- Blame
- Reproach
- Separation
- Depression
- Loss of Future Plans
- Guilt
- Shame
- Broken Trust
- Fear
- Temptation
- Physical Problems

Satan always seeks to multiply the consequences of sin in our lives! God wants to cancel out the power/effect of the consequences through forgiveness, cleansing, and fellowship.

<u>Pastor's Final Challenge</u>: Tonight we have taken care of our family business. No evil word is to be spoken or received by any of us from this time forward about this person(s) or this situation. If something ever comes up, remind anyone about tonight and that this was all handled correctly. Give a good testimony of God's grace at work in His people! That's our commitment to this person(s) tonight…Amen? Now, let's give God a praise clap offering for His goodness, forgiveness, and grace to us all!

<u>Call on someone to lead in prayer. Then encourage the people there to go to the Brother/Sister and give them a hug and express their love to them!</u>

Sometimes, it's wise to provide a recording of the service for the Brother/Sister and to ask their permission to share it with another in the future as an example.

CHAPTER 11

The Triangle of Leadership

L eadership is another important ingredient in building healthy relationships in the local church. My former Seminary Pastor and mentor for many years, Paul Burleson, once shared with me a simple concept that was a great help in relationship building among the Ministry Staff and Ministry teams where I pastored: "The Triangle of Leadership."

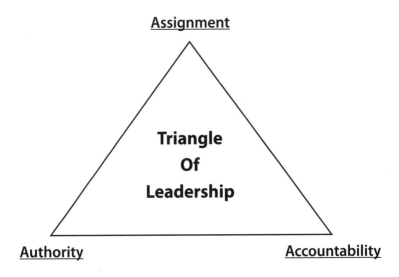

Assignment

Here's how the Triangle works. First, there is an *assignment* given to someone, whether it's an individual or a team. The assignment is a specific task or responsibility that is indicated by their role or title. For example, men are "called" to serve as Pastors in churches in various ministry areas including the Senior Pastor, or the Worship Pastor, or the Student Ministries Pastor, or the Missions Pastor, or the Discipleship Pastor, or the Family Ministries Pastor, etc. Laypeople are asked to assist these Pastors and serve on various Ministry Teams such as a Long-Range Team, or a Finance Team, or a Personnel Team.

The *assignment* is the task or position given to an individual or group by those in authority, whether that's an individual, team, or congregation. For example, a church may call a Pastor, but the Pastor alone may be given the authority to call his own Staff to serve in various ministry positions. It differs from church to church and from denomination to denomination.

What is especially important regarding the *assignment* is that there be a clear understanding or job description as to what the position, responsibility, or task entails. For most churches, there are clear instructions provided in their constitutions, bylaws, and team and personnel policies. These are imperative, not only for effective and fulfilling ministry, but for the sake of healthy relationships.

Nothing will so dampen or undermine relationships as a minister discovering a ministry expectation that he wasn't made aware of or a Team leader realizing there were things about his job that no one told him before he signed up. The *assignment* needs to be clearly communicated and agreed upon by those accepting it and also by those giving it.

Authority

Second, *authority* must be given to the person or persons with the assignment in order to do their job. Notice two arrows in the diagram representing this authority being given and received.

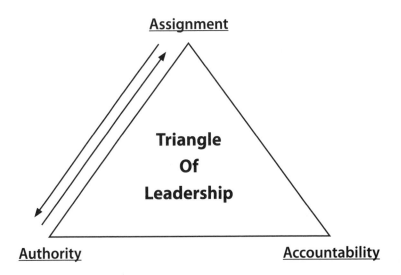

Whoever gives the assignment must also give the corresponding authority needed to carry it out. The authority received is never absolute. Only God has absolute authority. To be *under* authority is to properly serve with/in authority.

Sometimes the authority source is not just a person, group, or team. The source may also include the written and governing documents of the church.

Regardless, it is important to identify the proper source of authority and then grant authority to carry out the ministry or task. In other words, a person or team with a responsibility must also have the authority to carry it out. A person or team that has an *assignment*, but no *authority*, feels frustrated and unnecessary. This will cause relationship conflict.

In one of my pastorates, a wise businessman and respected church leader once told me, "Kent, we expect you and your Staff to do your jobs and make decisions for the church just like it is your business. I have a corporation to run. I don't want to make all the decisions for the church, too. Lead it, run it, and then call on people like me when it's necessary or required."

Too many churches have micro-managed their Pastor, ministers, and church members serving on Ministry Teams to death. To the contrary, some Pastors or ministers and members have abused the authority they received resulting in a more controlling church. Ideally, when people are given an assignment and the corresponding authority exists to carry it out, the context is one of low fear/high trust (not the opposite). The following third component of the Leadership Triangle helps maintain that type of atmosphere.

Accountability

The final leg of the Leadership Triangle is *accountability*. When people are given an *assignment* and the corresponding *authority*, they must understand there is always *accountability* for everyone. Again, only God is accountable to no one.

Pastors, Staff, and Team are all accountable. When they respect accountability and operate properly, they are "under" authority in a correct manner.

Is this principle important? There's a very interesting story in Matthew 8 where a centurion in the Roman army came to Jesus for the healing of his faithful servant. Jesus told the centurion, "I will come and heal him." (Matthew 8:7) The centurion objected and gave Jesus a very curious reply. He said, "No, I am not waiting for you to come under my roof. Just speak the word only, and my servant will be healed." (v.8) That's not the curious part; that's the *humble* part. It's what the centurion said next that is so intriguing. He said, "I am a man under *authority*, having soldiers under me. I say to this man, go, and he goes; and to another, come, and he comes; and to my servant, do this, and he does it." (v.9, emphasis added)

What was this man saying? He was saying as long as I am *under* authority, I am *in* authority, and I *have* authority. The centurion was accountable to someone; therefore, he could be accountable for others and for an assignment properly.

Jesus actually called what the centurion said "great faith." Why? Because the centurion was confessing his belief that Jesus was acting under His authority and according to His divine mandate and assignment. He knew this was where His power to heal came from! In other words, the centurion *believed* in Jesus.

Think about this again from the centurion's perspective. The centurion *knew* about authority, assignments or commissions, and accountability. Every Roman soldier and leader would know that. He just saw Jesus operating by the same principles except with a *higher* assignment, authority, and accountability. That realization convinced him that Jesus was divine.

Powerful Leadership

My point is this: the power for effective ministry and healthy relationships among those who serve together in the local church comes from a clear and defined *assignment*, a given and received *authority*, and an understood and maintained *accountability*. Let's look at some examples, and then let's add a practical dimension, too.

The Senior Pastor

Who is the Senior Pastor accountable to? What is his assignment? And what authority does he have? The answers depend upon each local church and can vary according to the size of the church Staff, but here's how it worked for me at my last church. Our Sunday school average was 300, Worship 350-400, and we had four full time Ministry Staff plus Support Staff.

Assignment:

To fulfill the Senior Pastor ministry duties spelled out in the constitution, bylaws, and policy manual which included: preaching, teaching, leading, counseling, caring, serving, visiting, and representing. This job description included vacation, "comp" and sick days, along with opportunities for continuing education. It also spoke to my character and personal spiritual walk.

Authority:

1. For the Pulpit – I could schedule guest speakers for the pulpit ministry of the church without approval.
2. For the Staff – I was to lead, develop, and evaluate the Staff annually.
3. I was an unofficial member of any Team or Committee.
4. I was in charge of the Support Staff.
5. I was the Chief Financial Officer for the church.
6. I was in charge of the overall church calendar coordination.

Accountability:

1. I was accountable first and foremost to the Word of God for my ministry and life.
2. I was then accountable to the constitution/bylaws/policies of the church in practice, in decisions, and in the general direction of the church. That document(s) was our daily "operating manual."
3. I was personally accountable to the Deacon Body for my pastoral ministry and was evaluated annually for edification and growth by the Deacon officers.
4. I worked with the Deacon Body regarding any matters pertaining to Ministry Staff.
5. I worked with the Personnel Team for any matters pertaining to the Support Staff.
6. The ultimate accountability for my ministry rested with the congregation, as Baptist churches are autonomous and operate by congregational rule.

For Staff members, Ministry Teams, and for the Senior Pastor also, there is a little "tool" that helps to facilitate this approach and keep the relationships and organization running smoothly. It's called "Regular" and "Crunch" decision-making. Let me illustrate. Let's say the Student Ministries Pastor wants to take the students to a nearby Youth Camp at Falls Creek in Oklahoma next year. Is this part of his assignment? Yes. Does he have the *authority* to decide which camp to attend? Yes. What/ Who is his *accountability?* In our church, the Senior Pastor was his accountability person. However, did he need to get permission from the Senior Pastor to make the decision on where the students would go to camp? No. The Youth Pastor only needed to make sure he stayed within the goals of the church for student ministry and youth camp, within the parameters of his given and approved budget, and within the proper dates and time on the church calendar approved by the Senior Pastor (who was responsible for the overall church calendar). This is an example of a "regular decision." He only needed to inform his Senior Pastor and check with him about the calendar.

However, what if the Student Pastor needed additional funds of $2,000 because the church camp he chose was located on the Gulf Coast of Florida and extra travel costs would be incurred? The decision then became what we called a "crunch decision."

In this case, the Senior Pastor needed to be involved in that decision before it was made. He might suggest the Student Pastor adjust his existing budget to make the Florida camp possible. The Student Pastor would have the authority over his budget to make that possible, and he could then inform the Senior Pastor of the choices he made.

Or, the Senior Pastor might value this request to the degree that he would go to the Finance Team and see if adjustments could be made in the overall church budget to approve this special request. If the Finance Team had this authority, they would make the final decision. This actually happened in our church, and the Finance Team made the decision, which was reported to the Deacon Body for accountability purposes. The decision was never reported to the congregation in a business meeting because it was not required by the congregation. This is the Triangle of Leadership at work. It's not perfect, but what a great tool!

**Remember: Regular Decisions – Inform Others
Crunch Decisions – Involve Others**

Over the years, Paul Burleson (who is now a Bible Conference Leader and Speaker) spoke in our church. Each time he would also meet with our present Staff and share this Triangle of Leadership tool.

On one occasion, our church held an orientation weekend for all the people serving on Ministry Teams for the next year. Paul shared many personal illustrations from his vast experience of pastoring churches of all sizes. He also answered practical and specific questions related to how the Triangle of Leadership works. As a result, our Ministry Teams entered the year with more fire and freedom than ever before, and we were able to share great unity and enthusiasm for the year ahead.

Senior Pastors

The Senior Pastor is involved in the Triangle of Leadership at almost every level, depending on the size of the church. He has a special relationship with the church that no other person shares. Therefore, it is imperative that he knows how to lead the way in forming and protecting healthy relationships in the church. That is what this next chapter is all about.

CHAPTER 12

That Special Relationship: Pastor and People

I have been truly blessed, I really have! In the two churches I pastored for a total of 23 years, we enjoyed a rich and wonderful *Pastor/People* relationship. I say I am "blessed" because I know of so many cases where this has not been true.

According to a study conducted by Lifeway Resources in Nashville, Tennessee a few years ago, more than 1,300 Staff members were dismissed in 2005.[37] Interestingly, relationship issues took the first five spots as causes or reasons identified with their dismissal. In that study, it was the general inability to "get along" that caused these Staff members of Southern Baptist churches to be terminated. Twenty-nine state conventions participated in the study. Of the 1,302 Staff members dismissed in 2005, 314 were bi-vocational, 655 were full-time Pastors, and 333 were full-time Staff.

The report went on to say that relational issues topped the list of causes for dismissal for 10 consecutive years (the only difference being their order from year to year). In truth, developing and maintaining healthy relationships in the church is a long-standing problem—especially among Staff leadership.

Of importance, too, is the fact that this information only represented the best data the study could gather on *forced* terminations. It did not include those who were pressured to resign.

The relationship "issues" cited in the Lifeway report included problems caused by everyone involved...the Pastor and the People. It was not just the Pastor who caused or had relationship issues. Sometimes it was the church leadership among the laity. We are all relationship-broken, challenged, and ill equipped in many local churches, and the growing number of forced terminations confirms it!

Older, seasoned Pastors often give young Pastors good advice for ministry, although the advice varies. E. V. Hill, the famed Los Angeles Pastor, would often tell young Pastors to observe three things to be successful:

1. Plow around the stumps.
2. Don't stop to slap a yapping dog.
3. Don't let anybody else raise your kids.

Anyone who has ever served any length of time in ministry would easily understand the truth and value in Dr. Hill's words, as well as the keen sense of humor. However, perhaps the best advice is something that has been repeated by many: "Preach the Word and love the people." You can't really improve on that, and there's a lot of wisdom in that single sentence of counsel for any Pastor. But what about some instruction from Scripture? What is the real crux of the matter for Pastors and People? I found a study of 1 Thessalonians 5:12-13 helpful when we apply its principles to the pastorate.

"Now we ask you, brothers, to respect those who work hard among you, who are over you in the Lord and who admonish you. Hold them in the highest regard in love because of their work. Live in peace with each other." (1 Thessalonians 5:12-13, NIV)

Look carefully at some of the words in this passage in order to gain a deeper understanding of its truth. Remember, Paul is writing to a young church with many new believers and very few experienced Christian leaders. He is obviously very concerned about the *Pastor/People* relationship because there is urgency in his words.

In context, Paul had just concluded some teaching on the end times, Second Coming, bodily resurrection, and death.

These were doctrinal matters. He closes out this epistle with guidelines and exhortations for practical application and personal relationships. Notice he begins with the *Pastor/People* relationship first, then moves to relationships with weaker, unruly, and fainthearted Christian believers and what type of ministry is to be rendered to them.

Pastor/People Relationship Instruction

- "Ask" – The word is translated "beseech" in the KJV and "request" in the NASV. In the NEB translation, the word "beg" is used. In whichever translation you use, this word is stronger than merely "asking." It is an earnestly felt exhortation, entreaty, and appeal. It is deeply felt by Paul and a strongly expressed petition.
- "Brothers" – This was Paul's favorite name for believers. He used it at least 60 times in his epistles and 27 times alone in 1 and 2 Thessalonians. Paul saw the Church as a family! A family needs leadership, and a family needs the right attitude towards leadership, whether it's God's family or our own. We need to consider what the right attitude and relationship with leaders looks like.
- "Respect" – The word is usually translated "to know" (as in the KJV), but in other translations it includes respect and appreciation. The meaning is to have a *relationship* and attitude of respect and appreciation for your leaders. Don't just express respect and appreciation from time to time. Have a relationship developed with these characteristics over time. If the relationship exists, the act or expression will follow. Why? How? Paul answers in the next key word below.
- "Work hard" / "Work" – It's the work itself the leaders are doing (and how hard they work at "the work") that results in respect and appreciation. Ministry work done right is never a "one day a week" job. Don't ever sarcastically complain or criticize that your minister "works only one day a week." That is disrespectful to God Himself who calls His Pastors. A Pastor who doesn't work hard may not be called and must be rebuked properly. (1 Timothy 5:19-20) The actual word "work" or "labor" alone is insufficient to describe what the Pastor does. It actually means, "to toil to the point of weariness and wear oneself out."

- "Over you in the Lord" – The NASV has a stronger translation: "have charge over you." It seems there is a responsibility implied here and somewhat of a spiritual authority. This principle can be taken too far, and it also cannot be taken far enough. Pastors are servant-*leaders* in a congregation, not hirelings employed to be demeaned by menial work only. They are to be God's men among the chosen plurality of leaders in a local church who give direction, insight, care, and leadership to the congregation as a whole.

- "Admonish" – The idea in this word is instruction, but instruction that rebukes wrong behavior or warns against something itself that is wrong. It seems to carry a suggestion of blame for wrongdoing.[38] It's also used in Acts 20:31. This is a tough part of a Pastor's job. It is best done in and through the ministry of the Word. Of course, this requires a proper handling of the Word. Years ago, a friend in ministry told me something about the Word of God being a two-edged sword, as it says in Hebrews. When it's in the hands of the Holy Spirit, it cuts and corrects like the two sides of a sharp filet knife. However, when it's in a man's hands alone, the listener feels the point, like being stabbed, poked, or attacked. That's a good distinction. In this day, the power of "positive thinking" is the name of the game for many preachers. However, it's clear from Paul here that the power of "negative thinking" can be healthy and needed, too, especially from a Pastor who has built good and genuine relationships with his people.

- "Hold them in highest regard" – Both the KJV and the NASV use one word for this phrase: "esteem." The word literally means "to value," and the Greek here is strong, representing a continuous attitude. One commentator wrote, "Do not esteem them because they are unusually fine looking, or because they are well dressed, or because they have such fine gifts of oratory. They should be esteemed because of the work they are doing."[39] In other words, those who value the work will value the worker, and the attitude and actions expressed toward a worker are a reflection of one's value of the work.

- "Live in peace with each other" – This final exhortation in verses 12 and 13 has an application to the *Pastor/People* relationship. God wants to bless His people and Pastors with peace between each other. Yes, it applies to the relationships among the Church as a whole, but that includes this primary relationship.

These two verses summarize the peace, harmony, joy, and health, that is made much more possible in personal relationships if there exists respect, value, responsibility, and a family-like perspective between Pastor and people.

There you have it. Just two verses, but they are packed with meaning and application to build and enhance one of the priority relationships in a local church...the relationship between the Pastor and his people! A Pastor's work also contributes to healthy relationships in the church, which is what we will study in this next chapter.

CHAPTER 13

The Pastor's Work and Healthy Relationships

B
eing able to lead and allowed to lead is a very important part of a Pastor's ministry. Let's take another look at our key passage from 1 Thessalonians from the previous chapter:

"Now we ask you, brothers, to respect those who work hard among you, who are over you in the Lord and who admonish you. Hold them in the highest regard ("esteem" KJV) in love because of their work. Live in peace with each other." – 1 Thessalonians 5:12-13

Dr. Leon Morris, commenting on the word "esteem" in verse 13, writes: "It is the duty of the church to do all they can to forward the <u>work</u> of the Pastor."[40] I agree, and I would add that doing so would immensely encourage and strengthen the relationship between Pastor and People. So, how can a church help a Pastor? Part of the answer concerns the area of the Pastor's leadership.

A Convention leader among Texas Baptists once said in my hearing that there is "nothing worse than a dictatorial leader…

except one who gives no leadership, or a congregation that won't allow him to lead." Most leadership experts today agree that everything "rises and falls upon leadership." If that is true, then a Pastor who does not know how to effectively lead or a church that refuses to let their Pastor lead are both seriously weakened by their own flaws. I believe part of the relationship problem between Pastors and People in many local churches today relates to the key area of leadership.

If I had to sum up a Pastor's job, I would use three words: Pastor, Preach, and Lead. Of these three, the most difficult part may be to lead. Think about it. If a Pastor will preach the Word in its entirety without compromise, and love his people in his sermons (not condemning or trying to control them), he will do just fine in the "Preaching" department.

If the same Pastor will attend and give oversight to the meeting of his people's needs, loving them in service, and being "there" for them in special times, he will be just fine in the "Pastoring" department.

However, it's in the "Leadership" department where the struggle often lies and where Pastors are most often hindered in fulfilling their calling. Leadership is where relationship conflicts occur. Instead of being used to the utmost by God in His work, he may feel limited because of weakness in this area. We must allow our Pastors to lead, not just pastor and preach. This is true for big churches and small churches alike.

Dr. Paul Powell once wrote, "Our preachers aren't dreaming anymore, and that's why the church overall is in such a nightmare."[41] I so agree, but I have a question. What good is dreaming if you are not allowed to lead?

Pastor Adrian Rogers once said, "A church should be Pastor-led, Committee-Accountable, Deacon-Served, and Congregation-Approved." That sounds like a good formula, if it all works together and if the leadership doesn't get bottled up in the process of accountability or approval. Too many times, however, our words sound right and our intentions are good, but the reality is far different.

Bill Hybels, in his book *Courageous Leadership*, calls leaders the "hope of the Church." While this is true, we need to enlarge the issue of leadership in the Church by addressing the fact that some churches don't know how to (or don't want to) let a pastor lead.

In answer to the leadership dilemma, here's a threefold suggestion I would like to make. Our Pastors need to be able to:
1. Lead with Authority. (1 Thessalonians 5:12, Hebrews 13:17)
2. Lead with Accountability. (1 Thessalonians 5:17-22, James 3:1)
3. Lead with Affirmation. (1 Thessalonians 5:13, 1 Timothy 5:17)

In this chapter, let's take a brief look at each truth.

Lead With Authority

Hebrews 13:17 NASV says, "Obey your leaders and submit to them, for they keep watch over your souls as those who will give an account. Let them do this with joy and not with grief…"

No one is suggesting this authority is absolute or without accountability. However, the verse does imply genuine responsibility and oversight for the leader and a respect and submissiveness for the believer.

It's hard to explain or understand the word "authority" today. The word has been so misused and abused that it's even thought of as distasteful and negative. Not only has the word itself fallen into disrepute both in society and in the Church, but the truth and the concept are misunderstood as well.

Think about the possible loss and harm this misrepresentation of authority might be causing in our culture today. Families in America are going in about a thousand different directions because of the chaos and confusion regarding who the clearly defined leader is supposed to be. Sometimes the leader is thought to be the dad. Sometimes it's the mom. Or, sometimes it's the in-laws, the kids, or the neighbors and friends, or even the television set! We've become a society who dislikes, distrusts, and rejects authority, and our homes have become very "dysfunctional" as a result. I realize this isn't the only problem in our homes, but it is a significant one, and maybe more so than we realize. God and His Word are not the authority they once were for many people.

The same scenario is oftentimes repeated inside the Church, God's Family. Many times today the *Pastor/People* relationship starts off with a very high fear/low trust commitment. It's almost like pre-nuptials are needed to protect both parties!

Perhaps we need to remember something. "Authority," as God defines it, is "good" and healthy. When God finished with all of creation, He said, "It is good!" This included the design for authority because He created that, too. Because of abuse, the pendulum has swung too far. Let me illustrate.

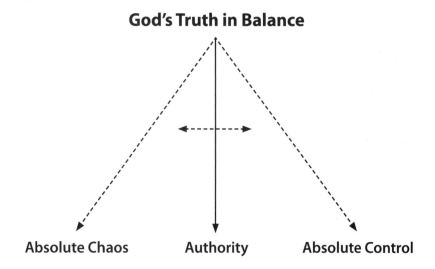

God's Truth in Balance

Absolute Chaos   **Authority**   **Absolute Control**

When God creates and gives a gift like authority to His people, it must be used and practiced in balance. Sometimes, however, people get out of balance and go to an extreme (in this case, absolute control). Once that occurs, a reaction will result. In time, the pendulum will swing all the way back in the opposite direction. The reaction doesn't typically restore "balance"; it only results in the opposite extreme.

Both extreme positions represent an abuse of God's truth and an abuse of God's people. They are equally out of balance. In the 1960s, America experienced a rebellion against the "establishment" and a rejection of all forms of authority. The Church was not immune to this cultural shift. Some of the reaction against authority in those days was very healthy and good. All races and genders were given a new respect and status, and we began to once again recognize and appreciate individuality. "Freedom" was the new theme, and although much abuse and damage occurred during that time, we experienced a lot of truth and balance as well. The dangers and the problems were the extremes.

Benefits of Authority

Honestly, we may have never completely returned to balance in regard to the issue of "authority." Maybe it's time to do so, especially for the Church. When God gave authority (for the government, church, and home), there were three good reasons for its use:

- Protection or Defense
- Provision or Development
- Purpose or Direction

Good leadership in balanced authority will produce these benefits. Think of Moses, for example, in the Old Testament. What if the people of Israel had only followed him without reservation or rebellion?

They accomplished so much just following as they did. However, one whole generation (including Moses himself) missed out on the Promised Land because the people did not submit to nor respect his leadership and authority.

Guarding the Church

Some people today try to "guard" their churches. One young but seasoned Pastor in his late thirties was told by a Deacon in a new church after his first year, "No matter how long you are here, we will never turn our church over to you." I can imagine that Pastor thinking to himself, "I wouldn't want it, even if you did."

But what did that Deacon *really* say? He was wise to be protective and responsible for the church, but he went too far. He was telling that new Pastor, "You are not the leader here, and you never will be." How wrong! Our leaders should come together, work together, and lead with authority together!

Lead with Accountability

Accountability is part of God's design and creation. No one has absolute authority apart from accountability except God. Here, too, there has been much abuse and misunderstanding of what the term actually means.

Accountability does not imply being someone's boss or telling him or her what to do. Accountability operates along clear lines of communication and cooperation. Accountability is positive, not negative. It is actually about freedom and responsibility, not control. Accountability is for the purpose of safety. Think of accountability like a baby crib. A baby crib has "bars" to keep the baby safe, not to hinder the freedom of movement (which would be dangerous). A baby is allowed to stick an arm or foot out of the crib, but not to fall out completely. The bars are healthy "boundaries," but not suppressing "bounds."

To evaluate your accountability guidelines in your church, ask yourself: Do they restrain and restrict? Or do they guide, protect, and facilitate?

I once heard Dr. John Maxwell compare authority to a great river. While it is within its banks, it is beautiful and useful. But when it overflows its boundaries, it destroys. Churches need to let the river flow…within its banks and boundaries.

Lead with Affirmation

Oh, how healthy affirmation is for leadership. People remember the encouragement they receive from others and the motivation it brings!

We can affirm others in different and meaningful ways, including:

- Words of Praise – Mark Twain once said, "I can live three months on a good compliment." Our modern culture is often sadly devoid of encouragement or praise. Everyone wants to criticize instead. Dr. Paul Powell wrote, "About once a century a person is ruined by praise, but every day a person is ruined by criticism."[42] In 1 Thessalonians 5:11, Paul writes believers to "encourage" and "edify" one another. Literally, the word "encourage" means "to strengthen someone by our words." Both words are present imperatives, meaning an obligation that is binding, continual, and habitual.[43]
- Words of Prayer – In 2 Corinthians 1:11, Paul said the local church "helped him by their prayers." (NASV, KJV) The word "help" pictures a group of workers side by side working to lift a load together that they could not lift individually.[44]
- Walk – Let our leaders see our Christian lives model love, hope, and faith, and they will rejoice. (1 Thessalonians 1:3, 7; 2:9, 20)
- Work – A people who know they are gifted and called for service and ministry will bless their leaders! (1 Thessalonians

1:3 reminds us to labor to the point of weariness, love to the point of self-giving.)

An Affirming Church

The last church I pastored was so affirming! They were consistent in sharing a good word, an encouraging thought, or a personal appreciation. I kept their notes and cards over the 13 years of ministry there. When we left, I had two large file folders full of their encouragement. Today, I cherish their expressions of affirmation. Dear people who are now in the presence of the Lord wrote many of the notes. However, their words "live" even to this day!

Shortly after we arrived at this church, my wife and I went driving one night. We ended up passing the church. Lights were on and cars were everywhere. My wife asked, "What's going on at our church?" I replied, "I don't know. I'm just the Pastor."

We soon learned our church was often like this, a beehive of activity. The people didn't need the Pastor there to be about their ministries. Throughout the time I served there, they took service seriously, and they were always about His work! You can't beat "affirmation" such as that!

Wouldn't it be great if churches had the opportunity to see what God can do when He uses others to lead His Church? Every church will see God in action when its leaders are allowed to lead with authority, accountability, and affirmation!

Leadership is not limited to Pastors alone. Next, we'll see how Deacons, Elders, or Lay Leaders are to use their leadership roles as the "keepers of the relationships" within the Church.

CHAPTER 14

Deacons: Point Men for Relationships

Deacons in Baptist churches have long been the object of some good-natured humor, but they've also been the target of some mixed sarcasm and criticism.

I heard a joke about a Pastor talking to little Susan in the hallway of their church following Sunday school. The Pastor asked Susan what she had learned that day. She replied, "We learned how to heal the sick and cast out deacons."

A friend of mine actually had the following happen to him one Sunday at the church where he served as Pastor. He was asked to teach some of the doctrines of the Church in a simple way to the elementary age children. He set aside several Sunday nights to do this. He got up in front of the class the first night and asked if anybody knew what baptism meant. He then talked about the Lord's Supper and grace, along with some other important subjects. One particular Sunday night, he asked the children if anybody knew what Deacons do. One little boy raised his hand and said, "I do! They break the bread, pass the wine, and tell the preacher when to resign!"

In all seriousness, I have never been in a church that didn't take a Deacon ordination as something very significant and reverent, and some of the finest Christian men I have ever known have worn that title, "Deacon."

My own father was a Deacon, and I know firsthand the kind of faithful service he rendered, the adversity he sometimes endured, and the challenges he undertook to serve the Lord and his church for many years. Dad knew good days and bad days in this ministry, but no one was ever more diligent, dedicated, prayerful, and consistent. I'm glad to say my Dad was a Baptist Deacon!

What Is a Deacon?

The word "deacon" literally means "through dust." It suggests a servant raising dust as he hastens to serve his master.[45]

According to Scripture, Deacons are to be:

Spiritually Mature	Acts 6:3, 5
Filled with the Spirit	Acts 6:3
Men of Wisdom	Acts 6:3
Men of Integrity without Question	1 Timothy 3:8, 10
Men of Exemplary Character	1 Timothy 3:8
Doctrinally Sound	1 Timothy 3:9
Visionaries	Acts 6:5
Kingdom Builders	Acts 1:8
Fellowship Builders	Acts 6:1
Ministry Providers	Acts 6:2

This is quite the list! This is a special group of men who render honor to the Lord, to their Pastor, and to their church just by their consistency of walk, positive attitude, commitment to spiritual growth, and faithful service.

In the passage believed to be the record of the first Deacon selections and service, Acts 6:1-7, we see unity for the fellowship of believers came as a result of their calling and ministry.

The church was exploding in membership—the term used for the first time in Acts 6 is "multiplication," which indicated exponential growth. Paul Powell writes, "However, with its unprecedented growth, the church was not keeping pace organizationally. Too many things were slipping through administrative cracks. Among them was adequate care for all the widows…What were the results of these first deacons being elected? Needs were served, conflict was settled, the apostles were freed to focus on their primary task, and the number of believers was multiplied greatly." [46]

RELATIONSHIP KEEPERS

In this way, we see how the Deacons' service and practical wisdom impacted relationships and provided the context for greater evangelism, ministry, and unity in God's Church! Perhaps there is a precedent here. Deacons have a "service" ministry obviously. But do they also have a problem-solving and *relationship-building* ministry too?

Point Men

I believe every member in every church should be challenged and reminded to be the "relationship keepers" for their local churches. However, Deacons have a special charge to take the lead in this area. They are the point men, leading by example to maintain the unity of the Spirit in their churches.

Somebody once said a long time ago, "There are givers and takers in life and you can be one or the other." President John F. Kennedy, in his inauguration speech, expressed a similar call when he said, "Ask not what your country can do for you. Ask what you can do for your country."

I want to suggest that Deacons be "contributors" in three special areas. The result will be healthier relationships and ministry in their local church.

Contribute to Love

Contribute to the love in the local church! That's at the top of my list. Years ago as a young Pastor, I was more concerned about "truth" than I was "love." Truth is important, very important. Isaiah 59:14 says, "Truth has stumbled in the streets." The prophet was writing about the nation of Israel and the deterioration of honesty, character, and integrity. It was a day of compromise, corruption, and judgment. America is no different today. Our society calls good, evil and evil, good. Truth, at least *God's* truth, isn't highly desired or valued. It is indeed a time for "truth" to be declared again!

But what I failed to recognize in those early years was the equal value and power of "love." Over time, I have since observed clearly what God can do in a church with members who really love one another!

Dr. Billy Graham is over ninety years old now. Once he was asked what he would do different in his ministry if he could. He mentioned three things. First, he would study and pray more and speak less. Second, he would spend more time with his family and less time on the road. Third, he would preach more about the love of God!

There is a Pastor I know in Houston, Texas whose church now averages over 6,000 in weekly attendance. For years, they depended upon billboards, newsprint, radio, and television to establish a public presence in the region. One year, this Pastor decided to change things. Instead of spending thousands of dollars on publicity, he announced to his people that for the rest of his ministry he was going to emphasize two things: Love God and Love People. The church followed their Pastor and embraced the same twofold commitment. Today, that Pastor, Dr. John Morgan of Sagemont Church, would tell you that this decision (and the follow through) launched their church to a greater level of growth and ministry than ever before.

Jesus said in John 13:35, "By this shall all men know you are my disciples (not my Deacons, preachers, church members), by your love (not your knowledge, talent, positions, or skills) for one another" (parentheses added).

Be honest! There are people in every church that are hard to love! There are even some people hard to like! But remember, the very ones hardest to "like or love" are really just like everyone else. Deep down, everybody wants to be loved. Some just make it hard for others to love them, and you have to work at loving them because it's worth it. And because it *will* make a difference in them, and in you, too!

How do we fulfill John 13:35? There are three things we can do.

- One, abide in the Lord daily. Let Him shed abroad in your heart the love of God for people by His Spirit. (Romans 5:5, Galatians 5:22)
- Two, get to know people. Don't let the "outward" side turn you off or turn you away. Sometimes love for others is something you have to *learn* as you get to know their hearts.
- Three, serve them through prayer and ministry. Service can melt and open up hard and calloused hearts. A "gift" often wins the heart of others!

Contribute to Leadership

The second thing Deacons can do to keep the relationships healthy and strong in the local church is to **contribute to the**

leadership. A line from the old James Garner movie says it well, "Support your local Sheriff."

One of the *best* things a Deacon can do for the Lord and for his church is to support his Pastor. Pastors aren't perfect (ask their wives), and we all know that Pastors make mistakes, sin, and are a continual "work in progress," just like everyone else. Pastors need accountability, prayer, honesty, forgiveness, and encouragement. A Pastor is never "above the law," so to speak, and must demonstrate responsibility. Some churches and Lay Leaders hesitate to hold their Pastor accountable for personal and professional growth. This is wrong for the church and for the Pastor or Staff Minister. However, if the Pastor is a good man, who loves the Lord, loves the people, and is faithful and true to God's Word, then Deacons need to lift him up and support him.

Pastors need to be treated with respect. Never call him names or talk about him negatively behind his back. Talk to him, in the *right* way at the *right* time, and in the proper place. Don't take "shots" at him in passing or in public. That's not acceptable, biblical, or Christian.

Think for a moment about that old story of Aaron and Hur in Exodus chapter 17, lifting up the arms of Moses. Honestly, I don't know why that passage is in the Bible. Maybe it's there to teach us about prayer and intercession as they relate to battle. But maybe, just maybe, it's there to teach us about leadership support, too.

The Israelites battled the Amalekites that day in the valley while Moses, Aaron, and Hur were on the mountain. Moses knelt, raised his arms, and prayed. As long as his arms were uplifted, the battle went the Israelites' way. When Moses grew tired and lowered his arms, the Amalekites started to succeed.

Aaron and Hur held up Moses' arms for how long? Until the battle was over and the victory was won. They endured!

In each church where I pastored for a total of 23 years, I faced pointed, heavy opposition from one key leader. And I faced significant pressure at home as my wife experienced severe health problems.

In each case, the great men who served as Deacons in those churches stood with me in battle, and they actually did several very practical things to let me do what only I could do as the Pastor. In essence, they "lifted up my arms," and it enabled us to weather the storms, move forward, and win some great victories in the Name of the Lord! It also enabled me to grow and mature personally and professionally. I thank God for these men!

Contribute to Life

Deacons can also **contribute to the life** in the local church! A local church has "life" in it, or it doesn't. People can tell the difference. Every Deacon and leader is important to this effort. A man can be a "Dead Sea" Deacon or he can be a "Sea of Galilee" Deacon. One just receives (like the Dead Sea with no outlet and no life in it), the other gives and receives (like the Sea of Galilee that is continually refreshed by the Jordan River). A "Dead Sea" Deacon is only a reservoir. A "Sea of Galilee" Deacon is a river. One person stops up the flow; the other has a river flowing through them.

"Life" is supposed to be flowing out of every believer. (John 7:37-38) Will the "life of God' in your church flow through you? Will you be a conduit, or will you dam it up and hold it back? It's flowing! The choice is yours.

Three things are important to keep the personal flow of life going. First, you must daily keep your personal life pure and holy in mind and body. When you aren't pure (and you can't get it that way quickly and easily) then step aside from leadership voluntarily.

When I was growing up, my family lived in San Antonio. We owned a Jeep and would often travel over five hours to my grandparents' home in East Texas. For some reason as a little boy, I once filled the Jeep's gas tank with dirt and debris. As we headed out, Dad had to stop every so often to flush the lines to the carburetor. Later, when I grew up and heard this story, I asked Dad if he had spanked me. He said he didn't spank me because he was so mad he thought he'd kill me! A clean heart, mind, and life are key to the flow of God's life in your just like clean lines are vital for a vehicle to run properly.

Second, your faith needs to be fresh and growing daily. It must be dynamic and real. The Bible says in Galatians 3:11, "We live by faith." Don't walk by your sight in your church; walk by your faith! (2 Corinthians 5:11) *Use* your sight, but don't live by it. Instead, live by faith!

Third, your ministry is key to your personal walk and "life" in a church. Deacons are called to serve and share. Somebody once said a Deacon is a light you put on a hill so that sailing ships know which way to go. Obviously, this person was confusing a Deacon with a beacon, but maybe that's not a bad definition for a Deacon either. A Deacon does not sit, soak, and sour. He serves and shares in such a way that others find The Way of Life through his ministry.

Be a ministry leader, not an office holder! Years ago, I attended a revival in a sister church to hear the guest preacher, a Pastor from Tennessee. He told us how a revival was happening in his church, and many people were being reached in the city of Memphis for Christ during those days. Naturally, the great numbers being saved caused the church members some inconvenience. One day at church, a Deacon walked up to the Pastor and said, "When are we going to get over this idea of trying to reach the whole city of Memphis?" About that time, an elderly lady walked by and said, "I hope it's not before my husband gets saved. He's still lost!" The Pastor smiled and didn't have to answer a word. The ministry of the church needs your support and your presence. Don't rock the boat; row it! Lead the way in ministry!

This is my charge to the men who serve as Deacons today. Be "contributors" to the Love, Leadership, and Life in your church. Do this, and you will build relationship bridges for "God and men" in your church, in your church's ministry, and people will come alive and be spiritually healthy!

CHAPTER 15

Staff: Makers or Breakers

Ihave depended upon older, more experienced Pastors a lot in my years of ministry. I once asked a seasoned veteran whom I greatly respected what his thoughts were about Ministry Staff personnel. Among the many other things he shared with me that day, he said one thing very clearly: "Staff can make or break you in ministry." How true were his words!

Since those days, I have gone through Staff hirings, firings, discipline, and blessings. I am grateful I can say that I count many, though not all, of the men I served with as some of my best friends today. They are literally my "brothers" in the battle, on the frontlines, for the Lord!

Honestly, though, this one specific relationship can either test or bless a Senior Pastor as much as anything else in local church ministry and service. It is also a relationship that has profound impact on a local church. It blesses a church to see Staff ministers united, genuine, loyal, loving, trusting, and growing together. When the opposite is true, it not only grieves that church Body but can also result in far worse.

Too many times, Pastors and Staff are careless or hurried in the hiring process. As an older Pastor shared with me, "It's much easier to hire a Staff member than to fire one." Too many times, Pastors and Staff communicate and coordinate poorly. Too many times, Pastors and Staff fail to build or prioritize their own friendships or working relationships. And, too many times, Pastors and Staff relate on a high fear/low trust level due to unrealistic expectations, selfish agendas, or a complete lack of teamwork training and understanding. This does not have to be the case!

Making the Change

To change things, this area of Staff Relationships and Teamwork must first be recognized for what it is: a major key to any church's health, ministry, or effectiveness. This is not a secondary issue or value, nor is it an optional or non-essential focus. This is a priority!

I have been amazed, and often saddened over the years, by the large number of Senior Pastors who do not give this area of ministry responsibility their serious and ongoing commitment. To a very real degree, "so goes the Staff, so goes the church!" I have been saddened also because I have known many highly competent and committed Staff members who longed for some kind of leadership, direction, and relationship with their Senior Pastor, but there was a void and lack of interest. To be frank, I would not recommend any church hire a prospective Senior Pastor without knowing of his Staff commitment, plans, and leadership model. Does he view Staff as his partners and team in ministry? Does he value Staff development and investment? Does he have a procedure for communication and coordination with his Staff? Will he be loyal to his Staff and be a learner, as well as a leader? Does he have a plan for annual Staff review and evaluation that is constructive and yet accountable?

In his book, *Leading At a Higher Level*, Ken Blanchard says, "Without teamwork skills, a person is unlikely to be successful."[47] Wow, that's pretty simple and straightforward! Teams, according to Blanchard, have the power to increase productivity and morale or destroy it. In your own experience, you've probably observed how strong, unified teams contribute to better decision-making, problem-solving, and greater creativity. Healthy teams also provide their members with self-worth and a sense of connection and meaning.

When it comes to teams, the "flexible" shall inherit the earth! A team that communicates well is better suited for handling the inevitable changes that come their way. In large part, it is up to the leadership of the team to impart recognition and appreciation for a job well done. Continual positive feedback is the lifeblood of any team, resulting in greater trust and (ultimately) more effective results.

Every Senior Pastor should desire to lead a strong, effective team with healthy growing relationships. This effort glorifies God, blesses a church, and grows each team member. Perhaps the place to start is for the Senior Pastor to hear what team members need from him. Among a list of suggestions that once appeared in Rick Warren's online Ministry Toolbox were ideas for connecting with Staff members.[48]

He suggested building relationships with Staff members and remembering to make regular visits to "their turf." Your presence at a special event or weekly activity can mean a lot for a Staff member to know you are interested in what they are doing. Encourage them to step out in faith in their ministry, confident of your support.

Again, it is also important to represent the Staff well before others, especially leaders in the church. This may mean watching out for their well being by advocating that the church provide adequate time away, continuing education credit, and/ or financial support for their families. You are shepherding the Staff as they shepherd others, and the example you set for them will be the example they model to their own volunteers. Chris Osborne, Pastor at Central Church in College Station, Texas, once mentioned that his Staff divides their days into thirds: morning, afternoon, and evening. All are expected to spend at least one third of each day with their family. He said simply, "We do not want to win the world and lose our families."

Staff Requirements

Leading Pastors over the years have suggested guidelines or "requirements" for healthy Staff relationships, resulting in effective personal and Church ministry. I found it helpful to share four principles with all incoming Staff members (both ministry staff and support staff). I also initiated an accountability structure for each principle.

1. **Positive Spirit**
   This is the ability to step back and see what God is teaching and how He is working in and through them...even in the most negative of situations. It stems from a great confidence in God.

2. **Loyal Spirit**
   This is the personal commitment not to speak or receive negative reports about a fellow Staff member until it has first been shared with him or her.
3. **Servant Spirit**
   This is the ability to be genuinely excited about making other Staff and church members a success. Lifting up and encouraging others for their benefit and not for personal gain is an important quality.
4. **Respectful Spirit**
   This is the desire to value the differences, opinions, thoughts, beliefs, and feelings of others and give them equal merit and worth.

   In discussing these requirements up front with the Staff, I let everyone know these were not optional. I also assured everyone that we would work faithfully to maintain them together. No one is perfect in keeping these guidelines; everyone fails. However, my goal was for the Staff to diligently strive to model these with each other before the Church Family as an example of the healthy relationship principles that are to exist among the members of the Body of Christ.

Staff Expectations

Every Senior Pastor also needs to work out his "standards" for his Staff and communicate them clearly. These, too, should be communicated at the very beginning of new staff hirings. Never leave your expectations to question or doubt. These may seem mundane, but to maintain healthy relationships and harmony in the church offices, they're important. It's the "little things" that often ruin relationships and weaken ministries. Here's a list of items to consider:
1. Schedules – Office Hours/Communication about Changes/ Availability/Accountability
2. Dress Code – Usual/Exceptions
3. Conferences – Required/Personal Selection
4. Friendships – Church/Staff
5. Job Performance
   - Get your job done or delegate it to be done.
   - Be a good time manager.

- Don't be a public complainer about the job, salary, schedule, etc.
- Be a friend and minister to other area ministers.
- Keep your word.
- Be a person of integrity—the reputation of the church is at stake. For example, return things on time.
- Plan ahead. Do the job early, not last minute.
- Be appreciative and considerate of the schedules of volunteers.
- Do not take outside jobs without first discussing with and gaining the support of the Senior Pastor.
- Produce! Count for Christ! Don't accept status quo, maintenance, or a certain level.
- Be responsible with church property and equipment.
- Be an example of a hard worker, not lazy or slothful.
6. Practice confidentiality.
7. Allow your spouse the freedom to serve in the church as he or she is led.
8. Be willing to adapt programs to meet needs.
9. The Pastor is in charge of worship services. Staff input is always included and valued.
10. The Church's Personnel Policy for Staff.
11. Annual Staff evaluations with the Pastor are for growth, goal-setting, etc.

Staff Evaluations

Churches of different sizes approach staff evaluations and reviews in different ways. Here are some sample questions that can be used to make this a constructive, profitable, and positive experience.

1. Honestly, what are your current strong points and weak points in your life or ministry leadership?
2. What could you do this coming year to help yourself grow, not just as a minister, but as a person?
3. Do you feel like your ministry is making progress, or are certain aspects stagnant? Why?
4. What steps could be taken to strengthen progress and remove stagnancy?
5. What has your personal devotional life been like the last three months?

6. Are you or your family facing any important health issues this year?
7. What's new in your work and what's *old?*
8. What books have you read this year? Significance? Application?
9. Evaluate your personal evangelism and visitation habits in the last six months.
10. Do you feel you have been effective with your personal time management?
11. Are there any changes or plans in your financial or family needs that you need to share?
12. What actions have you taken to strengthen your family relationships? Changes made? Changes needed?
13. Are there any projects, plans, or items you initiated but did not complete?
14. What ministry areas in our church do we as a Staff need to address?
15. What changes in communication, structure, or schedule would help you in your ministry this year?
16. Are there any suggestions you would make to improve Staff meetings, retreats, coordination, planning, or relationships?
17. What is the spiritual level of our church right now?
18. What are your ministry goals for this next year?
19. What do you dream about doing in ministry but hesitate?
20. Are there any items you want to discuss, but would rather not write about?   ___yes   ___no.

Team Players

Everybody on a Ministry Staff needs to be a "team player." People who refuse to adapt, sacrifice, support, or cooperate hurt the overall ministry. It can't be about "me" on a church Staff; it must be about "us." Talent, training, knowledge, or experience won't substitute for a team commitment and concept (ask any football coach!). Individualism, isolation, and independence are enemies of healthy relationships and powerful teamwork![49]

What is a team player?
* A team player is someone who is willing to join with others in doing special projects together for the ministry or benefit of the whole.

- A team player is someone willing to do projects or tasks not in their individual job description.
- A team player is someone who will give special time and effort over and above their expected responsibility or job requirement.
- A team player is someone who fulfills the mutually understood and agreed upon "personal" standards required for the successes of the team and the organization.
- A team player is someone who does their job with excellence, not allowing their assignment to fail the organization's standard, which would reflect upon and affect the other parts or whole of the organization.

Moral Accountability

Moral accountability is an area that a Ministry Staff team must address *together*. No minister can afford to overlook moral accountability. Guarding oneself takes work, attention, and teamwork. It's oftentimes awkward or inconvenient. But credibility, purity, and integrity are worth the price! The Elders of a church I know met monthly in pairs for encouragement, prayer, and accountability. The following questions were used:

- Have you been morally and sexually pure in all your relationships this month?
- Have you been reactive or proactive in relationships? If reactive, have you taken responsibility for your reaction and asked forgiveness if necessary?
- Have you maintained a clear relationship with God this month, including searching His Word regularly, dealing with sin in action or attitude, and in prayer seeking His face?
- Have you sought to share your faith with someone in need of the Gospel of Jesus Christ?
- Have you sought to walk in freedom financially, spiritually, and personally? If you have come into bondage in any way, do you wish to share it for direction and help?
- Have you answered honestly each of these questions?

Again I like Pastor Rick Warren's set of "Ten Commandments for Staff" that dealt with specific areas of moral accountability. He has openly shared them many times on podcasts and online in his blog. They bear repeating:

1. Thou shalt not go to lunch alone with the opposite sex.
2. Thou shalt not have the opposite sex pick you up or drive you places when it is just the two of you.
3. Thou shalt not kiss any attender of the opposite sex or show affection that could be questioned.
4. Thou shalt not visit the opposite sex alone at home.
5. Thou shalt not counsel the opposite sex alone at the office, and thou shalt not counsel the opposite sex more than once without that person's mate. Refer them.
6. Thou shalt not discuss detailed sexual problems with the opposite sex in counseling. Refer them.
7. Thou shalt not discuss your marriage problems with an attender of the opposite sex.
8. Thou shalt be careful in answering emails, instant messages, chat rooms, cards, or letters from the opposite sex.
9. Thou shalt make your co-worker your protective ally.
10. Thou shalt pray for the integrity of other staff members.

Remember, it will be the *relationship principles* and priorities exhibited by the Ministry Staff that "make or break" their leadership, their credibility, their ministry effectiveness, and their people's trust!

CHAPTER 16

The Four Letter Word!

One of the greatest generals in military history was Napoleon Bonaparte. Bonaparte was made a full general at age twenty-six. He used shrewd strategy, bold cunning, and lightning speed to his advantage to win many victories. The Duke of Wellington, one of the general's most formidable enemies, said, "I consider Napoleon's presence in the field to equal forty thousand men in the balance."[50]

Napoleon was once quoted as saying this about Jesus Christ: "I know men, and I tell you that Jesus Christ is not a man. Alexander, Caesar, Charlemagne, and myself have founded great empires: but upon what did these creations of our genius depend? Upon force. Jesus alone founded His empire upon love, and to this very day, millions would die for Him."[51]

In 1965, a song by Hal David and made popular by Burt Bacharach was entitled, "What the World Needs Now Is Love." Of course, the Lord knows this is what the world needs, and He gave to His people, the Church, the greatest example, experience, expression, explanation, and empowerment of love that will ever exist. This idea is presented throughout Scripture:

The Greatest Example
"Dear friends, let us love one another, for love comes from God. Whoever does not love, does not know God, because **God is love**." (1 John 4:7-8 NIV) Have you ever known a parent, a grandparent, a relative, or a friend who seemed just "full of love"? How could you not love them in return? That's who God is!

The Greatest Experience
"We love because He loved us." (1 John 4:19)
"And I pray that you, being rooted and established in love, may have power, together with all the saints, to *grasp* how wide and long and high and deep is the love of Christ, and to *know* this love that surpasses knowledge." (Ephesians 3:17b-19a)
It's one thing to know the *fact* of being loved; it's another to know the actual *feeling* of being loved.

The Greatest Expression
"This is how we know what love is: Jesus Christ laid down his life for us." (1 John 3:16 NIV) Love is shown and given to others! Love is not just a noun; it's a verb.

The Greatest Explanation
1 Corinthians 13, the "Love Chapter." What more can I say? Within these words is the very description of Jesus' character...the greatest explanation of love to a world struggling to define what love really is.

The Greatest Empowerment
"But the fruit of the Spirit is love ..." (Galatians 5:22)
Love *from* God and the love *of* God is a spiritual fruit. It is not natural.

The World Needs Love
Yes, the world does need love, and God has sent it to us through the Scriptures, through His Son, and through His Spirit. He now seeks to send it through His Church! No wonder healthy, loving relationships between Christians are so important in the Bible. The Church is to be the reservoir and river of God's love to the world!

What a miracle genuine love in the Church can be.

Christians are to demonstrate they are Christians by their love for *one another* (John 13:35). Not through their professed love for God, as perceived by their Bible knowledge, study, generosity, devotion, or religious activity (as great as it might seem).

It's our love for *brothers and sisters* in Christ, with whom we have nothing else in common sometimes. It's love for those with totally different backgrounds, personalities, temperaments, social standing, or race that gets the world's attention. It's love for those who have demonstrated prejudices or have experienced miserable failures that makes them notice. It's love for those we worship with, serve with, learn with, and do "church" with that reveals our identity as Christ-followers to a watching world.

And yet, it's because God's people have received and experienced His love for themselves that they can indeed become an oasis of love for one in need and an ocean of love for those outside the Church.

Bill Gaither wrote a song entitled, "I Am Loved!" that talks about being willing to love others simply because God loved us first. People usually give from what they have received. In 1998, the *Dallas Morning News* contained an article on prison inmates.[52] The article revealed that almost half of female inmates and 13% of male inmates in local jails have been abused at least once. It addressed the cycle of violence that begins with victims and ends with the victims becoming the victimizers. However, there is hope for breaking this cycle. Dr. Karl Meninger, the famed psychiatrist, called love the "medicine" the whole world needs and even claimed learning to give and receive love would heal many physical and mental conditions.

If that is true, then the local church should be the number one healing agent in the world! The Church has been "given much," and therefore "much is required." (Luke 12:48) The Church has received love, acceptance, forgiveness, mercy, grace, goodness, joy, and peace. Oh, that the Church would pour these out on the world today with a broken and grateful heart!

Someone once said, "Great Christians are great receivers." The idea was our pride sometimes keeps us from receiving from God all that He would give. Once we humble ourselves, we receive those things God can give. That enables us to become "great" Christians. It's then that Christians can become great givers as they minister to others from the blessings and grace they received!

The Power of Love

Christians haven't fully realized all they have been given. Somebody once said, "Jesus is the only gift that men have received and not yet fully unwrapped."

Years ago when I graduated from college and headed off to Seminary, I put all my earthly possessions into a small, light blue Ford Maverick. For most of my life, I had lived in small towns, even while attending a Baptist college. My seminary was located in the metroplex of Fort Worth and Dallas. As I drove into Dallas that day on my way to Fort Worth, it was pretty overwhelming and lonely. I felt very small and very insecure. I arrived at Southwestern Seminary knowing only a handful of people who had graduated from the same Baptist college a year or two before me.

I found my way to the campus, parked my car, and went into a crowded Administration office. I had been accepted as a student and was supposed to have a dorm room assignment waiting for me. But something had happened. The "Jesus Movement" of the sixties and early seventies had resulted in hundreds, maybe thousands of students sensing God's call into vocational ministry. Many were seeking a Seminary education. Later, one of my professors explained that Southwestern found itself facing an immediate need for a 10-year acceleration of all their future planning regarding classrooms, teachers, and housing. For me and for hundreds of others, there was simply "no room in the inn." That day I was put on a waiting list and told to search for a private apartment off campus in which to live for the meantime. This news left me feeling even more lost, bewildered, and stunned. One couple from my college days came to mind, and I decided to call them first for help. I just needed a friend to talk to and a place to stay for a few nights. I really had no other place to turn.

When I called my friend, what a surprise was waiting for me. I told him about my plight and his reply was, "Kent, no problem, we've been expecting you." It seems they knew in advance of the overcrowding problems. When I called, they had already decided to offer their couch as a temporary place for me to stay for as long as I needed!

Later that night, another former college friend came by. As we all talked, I shared how all my plans were up in the air. Not knowing anyone, I didn't know where to begin to solve this problem.

Things were all happening so fast. There had been no forewarning from the Seminary to any of us incoming first-year students.

At that point, my friend said something to me that I have never forgotten. He sensed my need, fears, and anxieties. He looked me square in the eyes and made sure I heard him say, "Kent, if you just knew how much God loves you, you wouldn't be worried about a thing." He even repeated those words to me again, making sure I received this message and didn't just "hear" the words.

I did hear, too. I knew intellectually of God's love and had "heard" that truth all my life. I think it was the first time that I really experienced and felt overwhelmed by the reality of God's love for me personally.

Everything worked out at Seminary with the housing needs, just like it always does. However, I will never forget the moment I knew in my heart, not just in my head, that God loves me! Perhaps this is part of what the Church in every generation needs to know for real. Maybe, if we could "receive" this message in truth, we could then set about building the healthy relationships that would allow the Church to do ministry more effectively than ever before in the history of the Church. That's my prayer! I think it was Jesus' too (John 17).

RELATIONSHIPS...the most important word in the English language. Let's make the main thing, the main thing!

Notes

[1] Oscar Thompson, *Concentric Circles of Concern* (Nashville: Broadman Press, 1981), page 15.

[2] Ibid., page 21.

[3] Ibid., pages 24-27

[4] Mark Gerzon, *Leading Through Conflict* (Boston: Harvard Business School Press, 2006), pages 1-3.

[5] George Barna, as cited in *Revival Report* by Life Action Ministries, February, 1998.

[6] John C. Maxwell, *The 360° Leader* (Nashville: Thomas Nelson Publishers, 2005) page 119.

[7] Rick Warren, *The Purpose Driven Church* (Grand Rapids: Zondervan, 1995), pages 102-103, 340.

[8] Chip Ingram, *Good To Great In God's Eyes* (Grand Rapids: Baker Books, 2007), page 54.

[9] Jack MacGorman, *The Gifts of the Spirit* (Nashville: Broadman Press, 1974), pages 31-32.

[10] Ibid., pages 47-48.

[11] Jim Putman, *Church is a Team Sport* (Grand Rapids: Baker Books, 2008), page 12.

[12] Ibid., page 31.

[13] Ibid., page 32.

[14] Ibid., pages 62-63.

[15] As cited by Gerzon, page 49.

[16] Larry Julian, *God Is My CEO* (Avon: Adams Media, 2002), pages 97-98

[17] Ibid., page 108.

[18] Ken Blanchard, *Leading At A Higher Level* (Upper Saddle River: FT Press, 2007), pages xxi and 268.

[19] Warren Wiersbe, *The Bible Exposition Commentary* (Wheaton: Victor Books, 1989), page 248.

[20] Ibid.

[21] Duane Litfin, *The Bible Knowledge Commentary*, New Testament Edition (Wheaton: Victor Books, 1983), pages 755-756.

[22] As cited by Gerzon, page 167.

[23] *New York Times*, June 7, 2004 as cited by Gerzon, page 154.

[24] Gerzon, page 55.

[25] Ingram, page 46.

[26] John Maxwell, *Developing The Leader Within You* (Nashville: Thomas Nelson Publishers, 1993), page 125.

[27] Gregory Morris, *In Pursuit of Leadership* (Longwood: Xulon Press, 2006), page 73.

[28] Henry Wadsworth Longfellow, as cited by Albert M. Wells, Jr., *Inspiring Quotations* (Nashville: Thomas Nelson Publishers, 1988), page 98.

[29] Morris, page 122.

[30] Maxwell, *360° Leader*, page 101.

[31] Frederick F. Reichheld, *Loyalty Rules* (Boston: Harvard Business School Press, 2001), page 2.

[32] Morris, page 77.

[33] Ibid., page 129.

[34] Maxwell, *Developing the Leader Within You*, pages 124-125.

[35] Blanchard, pages 159-161.

[36] J. W. MacGorman, "The Discipline of the Church," in The People of God: Essays on the Believers' Church, ed. Paul A. Basden and David S. Dockery (Nashville: Broadman and Holman, 1991).

[37] http://www.lifeway.com/article/1634711

[38] Leon Morris, *The Epistles of Paul to the Thessalonians* (Grand Rapids: Eerdman's Publishing Co., 1979), page 99.

[39] John Walwoord, *The Thessalonian Epistles*, *Bible Study Commentary* (Grand Rapids: Zondervan Publishing House, 1976), page 58.

[40] Leon Morris, page 99.

[41] Paul Powell, *The New Minister's Manual* (Dallas: Annuity Board of the Southern Baptist Convention, 1994), page 89.

[42] Paul Powell, *True Confessions of a Preacher* (No publisher given, 1977), page 69.

[43] Johnny Draper, *1 and 2 Thessalonians – The Hope of a Waiting Church* (Wheaton: Tyndale House Publishers, 1979), page 142.

[44] Powell, *Minister's Manual*, page 94.

[45] Paul A. Meigs, *The Office of the Deacon as Given in the New Testament* (Published by the Florida Baptist Convention, undated).

[46] Paul Powell, *The Church Today* (Dallas: Annuity Board of the Southern Baptist Convention, 1997), pages 165, 169.

[47] Blanchard, page 167.

[48] http://pastors.com/, Rick Warren's Toolbox email resource, July 3, 2007.

[49] There are two books by Dr. John Maxwell that every minister, no matter the size of their church or Staff, ought to read: *The 360° Leader* and *The 17 Essential Qualities of a Team Player*

[50] John C. Maxwell, *The 17 Essential Qualities of a Team Player* (Nashville: Thomas Nelson Publishers, 2002), page 9.

[51] Ravi Zacharias, *Jesus Among Other Gods* (Nashville: W. Publishing Group, 2000), page 148.

[52] *Dallas Morning News*, April 27, 1998

Bibliography

Blanchard, Ken, *Leading At a Higher Level*. Upper Saddle River, New Jersey: FT Press, 2007.

Draper, Jimmy, *The Hope of a Waiting Church*. Wheaton, Illinois: Tyndale House Publishers, 1979.

Gerzon, Mark, *Leading Through Conflict*. Boston, Massachusetts: Harvard Business School Publishing, 2006.

Ingram, Chip, *Good to Great in God's Eyes*. Grand Rapids, Michigan: Baker Books, 2007.

Julian, Larry, *God Is My CEO*. Avon, Maine: Adams Media, 2002.

Kouzes, James J. and Posner, Barry Z., *Credibility*. San Francisco, California: Josey-Bass Publishing, 2003.

Litfin, Duane, *The Bible Knowledge Commentary (2 Timothy)*. Wheaton, Illinois: Victor Books, 1983.

MacGorman, Jack, *The Gifts of the Spirit*. Nashville, Tennessee: Broadman Press, 1974.

Maxwell, John C., *Developing The Leader Within You*. Nashville, Tennessee: Thomas Nelson Publishers, 1993.

Maxwell, John C., *The 17 Essential Qualities of a Team Player*. Nashville, Tennessee: Thomas Nelson, Inc., 2002.

Maxwell, John C., *The 360° Leader*. Nashville, Tennessee: Thomas Nelson Publishers, 2005.

Meigs, Paul A., *The Office of Deacon as Given in the New Testament*, Published by the Florida Baptist Convention, undated.

Morris, Gregory T., *In Pursuit of Leadership*. Longwood, Florida: Xulon Press, 2006.

Morris, Leon, *The Epistles of Paul to the Thessalonians*, Grand Rapids, Michigan: Eerdman's Publishing, 1979.

Powell, Paul, *True Confessions of a Preacher*. No publisher given, 1977.

Powell, Paul, *The New Minister's Manual*. Dallas, Texas: Annuity Board of the SBC, 1994.

Powell, Paul, *The Church Today*. Dallas, Texas: Annuity Board of the SBC, 1997.

Putman, Jim, *Church Is A Team Sport*. Grand Rapids, Michigan: Baker Books, 2008.

Reichheld, Frederick F., *Loyalty Rules*. Boston, Massachusetts: Harvard Business School Press, 2001.

Thompson, Oscar, *Concentric Circles of Concern*. Nashville, Tennessee: Broadman Press, 1981.

Walwoord, John, *The Thessalonian Epistles, Bible Study Commentary*. Grand Rapids, Michigan: Zondervan Publishing, 1976.

Warren, Rick, *The Purpose Driven Church*. Grand Rapids, Michigan: Zondervan, 1995.

Wells, Albert M., Jr., *Inspiring Quotations*. Nashville, Tennessee: Thomas Nelson Publishers, 1988.

Wiersbe, Warren, *The Bible Exposition Commentary*. Wheaton, Illinois: Victor Books, 1989.

Zacharias, Ravi, *Jesus Among Other Gods*. Nashville, Tennessee: W. Publishing Group, 2000.